# THE SUSSEX PLAN

## SECRET WAR IN OCCUPIED FRANCE
### IN FRANCE COVERT OPERATIONS

## 1943-1944

Dominique SOULIER

Histoire & Collections

# CONTENTS

SOLDIER'S PAY BOOK (ACTIVE)
(SERVICE)
ARMY BOOK 64 (PART II)

my Number ...........7944........
ame (block letters) .......B.O.V. LEMAN G.........
an Names in full ...........................

— Corps......B.E.C.R.A...........
NIT MUST NOT BE ENTERED.

Instructions to Soldier

ce this book whenever you require an
n account, or when instructed to do so.
ceipt, on the acquitance roll of the
for all cash advances made to you.
the payment will sign the corre-
ook on the page for cash payments.
book except to sign your
ber on pages 7, 9, 11

II at once report the loss
en a new book will be
erstood that no pay can
efore the date on which
balance has been ascer-

formation on pages

*Close-up view on Jacques Coulon's, a.k.a "Ollivier", service jacket. As an exception to normal Free French uniform regulations, Sussex agents were authorized the wear of US Army walking out uniforms. (Sussex picture collection)*

# A HIGHLY SECRET PLAN

The Sussex plan was shrouded in secrecy. Even though they had followed the same training, and regardless of the region where they operated, the men and women who were parachuted or landed in occupied France were in theory not supposed to get in contact with the résistance movements once they had parted with their reception committee.

Many information contained in this book originate from the NARA American archives. Half of the Sussex missions were carried out in support of American services (OSS). The other half was performed with British services, namely the MI 6. British archives and post mission reports of the "Brissex" missions are still protected by the official Secret Act. Thus, this book contains more information about the American side of Sussex (OSSEX) than about the British side.

At the end of the Seventies, the Plan Sussex Old Comrades Association had planned to produce a book, which would have presented the different missions and gathered the testimonies of the former agents under one cover. This book has never seen the light of the day.

Several decades later, Dominique Soulier, having inherited the archives of the Association, found a treasure throve of documents, particularly a text called "Un certain Louis Bonnet" written by Jean-Jacques Schumacher. Several paragraphs of that text are used in this book to illustrate the "Berthier" mission.

In order to pay tribute to those women and men, the author decided to write this book.

At the current Museum, the Musée du Plan Sussex in Hochfelden, France, where all the artefacts pictured in this book are exposed until the end of 2013, most visitors are astonished when they discover the extraordinary story of the Sussex plan and when they realise the risks its agents were running. The visitors also discover the key role the Sussex plan played in the success of Operation Overlord.

All these artefacts, most of them donated by former Plan Sussex agents or their families will be exposed, from the beginning of 2014 in the new "Musée Technique et Militaire 1939-1945" located in La Wantzenau, North of Strasbourg.

After a first book named "Le Plan Sussex Très Secret" published by Editions Hirlé, this second volume dedicated to these highly covert missions focuses more on the equipment and documents used by the agents. As mentioned previously, all these artefacts are part of the permanent collections of the Musée du Pays de La Zorn located in Hochfelden in Alsace.

# 1943

# WHY WAS SUCH AN OPERATION EVER LAUNCHED?

In 1943, the main résistance networks that were operating inside occupied France had been severely hit by the German counter intelligence effort and they would continue to suffer cruel losses until the end of the occupation. Among the best-known networks were the Confrérie Notre-Dame (CND), Castille, F2, Saint-Jacques, Alliance, Brutus, Phratrie, Hunter, Ajax, Marco Polo, Cohors, etc. Several of those networks were almost destroyed by the combined action of the Gestapo and the Abwehr and hundreds of patriots were arrested, tortured, deported or executed.

Moreover, and because of the infiltration of some intelligence gathering networks by double agents, the reliability of the intelligence gathered was no longer certain. The ferocity of the German counter intelligence operations was

such that General Eisenhower's SHAEF staff started fearing that not enough résistance networks would still be operational when most needed, i.e. before and just after D-day.

In order to mitigate that problem, the combined staff had reached an agreement with General de Gaulle. Roughly a hundred Free French agents would be seconded to the British and American services. This solution was chosen, as it was obvious that only native Frenchmen and women would be able to fit inconspicuously in the population of occupied France, either as part of a network or within a maquis. During that period, not being able to speak French like a native or looking "un-French" would have led to certain arrest.

Thus, the Sussex plan was born.

In order to carry out the agreed plan, the American OSS and the British SIS needed the help of the Free French in general and of the BCRA (the London-based Free French secret services) in particular in order to recruit French officers capable of being deployed on such missions.

"Colonel Passy" (André Dewavrin DSO, MC), the head of the BCRA, played a key role in the creation of this operation; considering the importance of the goals, traditional service rivalry were forgotten and team spirit prevailed. The Sussex plan was given a tripartite command under the orders of Commander Kenneth Cohen CB, CMG of the British Secret Intelligence Service (SIS). His deputies were lieutenant-colonel Francis Pickens Miller OBE of the OSS and Gilbert Renault DSO, OBE, a.k.a "colonel Rémy" of the BCRA.

*Above.*
**Commander Kenneth Cohen CB, CMG, SIS, in charge of the Plan Sussex.**
*(The Estate of Kenneth Cohen picture)*

*Opposite.*
**Gilbert Renault DSO, OBE, a.k.a "colonel Rémy".**
**He took an active part in the recruiting of each Sussex agent. This picture was dedicated to Guy Wingate.**
*(Sussex picture collection)*

# CHRONOLOGY

**AUTUMN 1942**
beginning of the first staff talks

**JULY 1943**
the main American instructors and officers were recruited in the USA

**MID-SEPTEMBER 1943**
Lieutenant-Colonel Francis Pickens Miller and Major Justin O'Brien arrived in London from Washington DC

**22 OCTOBER 1943**
the first French volunteers arrived in London

**30 OCTOBER 1943**
Free France accepted to take part in plan Sussex

**13 NOVEMBER 1943**
In Saint Albans, establishment of "TS 7" school and arrival of the British and American instructors

**23 DÉCEMBER 1943**
the agent selection committee arrived in French North Africa

**1ᵉʳ JANUARY 1944**
32 agents started training in the United Kingdom

**5 JANUARY 1944**
the first "Pathfinder" team was created

**8 FEBRUARY 1944**
the "Pathfinder" team was parachuted over occupied France

**15 MARCH 1944**
106 agents were on training

**17 MARCH 1944**
the last agents were recruited in French North Africa and in the United Kingdom

**9 APRIL 1944**
the first three teams were parachuted, "Berthier", "Drolot", "Plainchant"

**END OF SEPTEMBER 1944**
reception of the last message from a deployed team; all the teams ordered to return to Paris and then London.

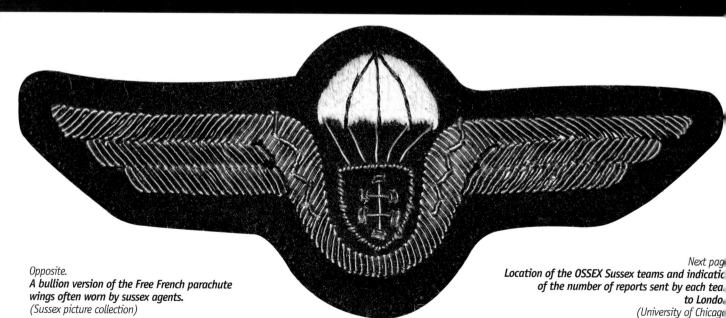

*Opposite.*
*A bullion version of the Free French parachute wings often worn by sussex agents.*
*(Sussex picture collection)*

*Next pag[e]*
*Location of the OSSEX Sussex teams and indicati[on]*
*of the number of reports sent by each tea[m]*
*to Londo[n]*
*(University of Chicag[o]*

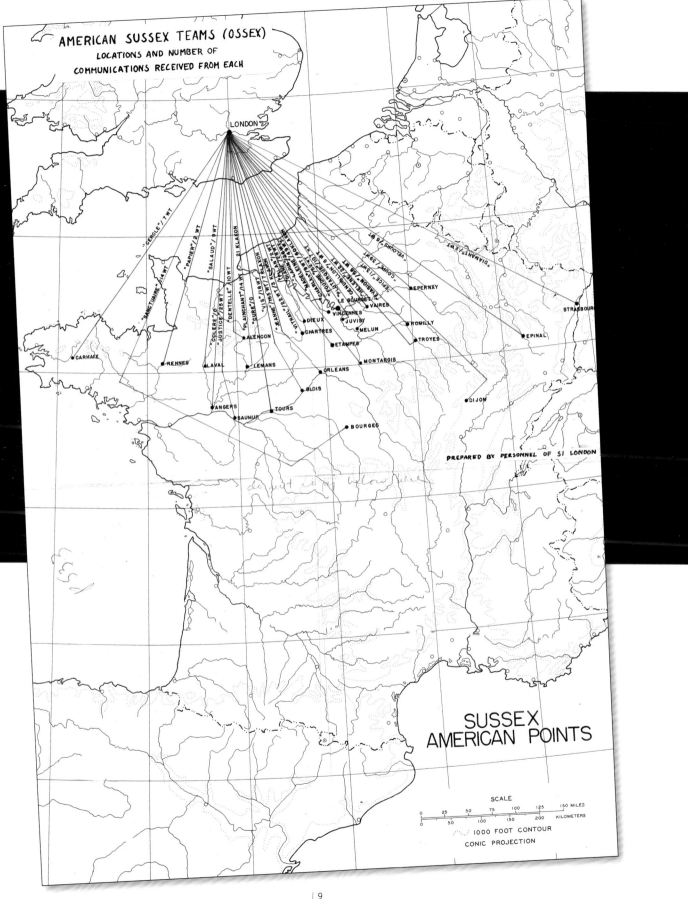

# RECRUITING SUSSEX AGENTS

"RÉMY" MANAGED TO PERSUADE GENERAL DE GAULLE to let him pick his own men from the ranks of the French armed forces under the supervision of "colonel Saint-Jacques", a.k.a Maurice Duclos. The teams were thus established in this way and de Gaulle scored one final victory over the intelligence services of his rival General Giraud and over his old enemy Robert Murphy who had done his best to try and favour Giraud's SR (Services de Renseignement or intelligence services) over his own.

A total of 120 "Sussex" agents were selected; of those, 108 were finally parachuted over occupied France. Some agents performed more than just one mission; only four were more than 30 of age; the other were between 17 and 26 ; and finally, two of those agents were women.

The Sussex plan had identified 53 areas of interest in occupied France between the tip of the Finistère in Brittany to the border with Belgium and the East of the country. Each of those areas was to be investigated by a two-man team (an observer and a radio operator) operating in civilian clothes. Their mission was to report on all enemy activities in their area of interest to the combined staff.

Initially, the idea had been to drop those teams "blind", that is without a reception committee

*Next page.*
*In November 1942 when American forces landed in French North Africa, many of the future Sussex agents were stationed there. Most were serving in army units such as the Spahis (North African light cavalry) or tirailleurs (locally recruited rifle units) but some also came from Navy of Air Force units based in Algeria, Morocco or Tunisia.*
*(ECPAD picture)*

and solely on the basis of information gathered through air reconnaissance missions. "Colonel Rémy" was strongly opposed to that idea, arguing that the casualty rate of such parachute operations would be unbearable. Luckily for the agents, his voice was heard and the agents were not dropped "blind".

French agents were recruited from all the branches of the armed forces (army, navy, air force), in the two Free French divisions as well as in the French North Africa-based «Armée d'Afrique». Some volunteers had managed to escape from occupied France, some by sea and some having had to spent some months in the dreadful Miranda camp in Spain but on the whole, most volunteers came from units based in French North Africa. All of them knew how to behave in occupied France.

During their selection process, they were subjected to various exams and test that had been perfected by the American and British services over the years. They also had to endure severe questioning in order to test their motivation and to understand whether they would perform adequately in the field. In his book Souvenirs, Georges Soulier, who was then part of the 2e régiment de Spahis algériens (2ᵉ RSA, an indigenous light cavalry unit of the French Armée d'Afrique), gave some details of this entirely new for him process.

*"I was sent to Algiers with another three of my friends from the same regiment who had volunteered just like me. We were accommodated in a private flat and then we had to go through several written exams. This was entirely new for us as this*

*Opposite.*
**Georges Soulier in his**
**2°Régiment de Spahis**
**(2ᵉ RSA) uniform in Tlemcen**
**in 1942.**
*(Sussex picture collection)*

*Below.*
**Prae Wood House in St Albans was the second manor**
**where Sussex agents were housed while in training.**
**Two other huts, not visible on that picture, were also**
**used for the same purpose.**
*(Sussex picture collection)*

way of selecting people was not common in France. The next day, I was summoned into an office where I was faced with two men dressed in civilian clothes. One spoke very good French but with a thick American accent which gave him straight away. The other one was a native Frenchman. I did not know him but latter when I was part of the service I met him again and then realised he was "Colonel Rémy".

I went through a very close interrogation, not only on my résumé but also on a multitude of information about me, my childhood, my parents, my brothers, my sisters, my friends etc. They had to know everything about me. They were asking for the weirdest information; for example, they asked me what age was I when I went to school for the first time, in what school, what was my temper at the time and if I had a tendency to chat a lot. Luckily for me, the only prize I received in kindergarten was for being the quietest child! I told them so and it looked like they liked to hear that. They also asked me about my studies, my hobbies, the kind of books I liked to read etc. After several hours of such interrogation, "Rémy" gave me some indications on what would be expected of me. After specialised training

in the United Kingdom, I was to be parachuted over occupied France and conduct an intelligence-gathering mission in support of the allied staff in order to prepare the forthcoming landing of allied forces in France.

He insisted on the dangers of such a mission. Those dangers would be all the more severe that I would operate in civilian clothes and not in uniform; if I was to be arrested, I would not be considered as a prisoner of war and I would probably be first tortured in order for me to confess everything I knew about the service and my mission and then shot. "Rémy" then asked me if, after those details, I was still interested in volunteering. Of course, such a prospect gave food for thoughts but I told myself that I was not sure of being caught and that anyway I had not joined the armed forces to stay idle. Moreover, such activities seemed to be positively fascinating so I answered yes.

"Rémy" then told me I should now consider myself a BCRA agent. As such, for my and my families' own good, I was to change identity. He told me I now was called "Alain Wallon". I would soon be issued with new identity papers. He then insisted *on the fact that our meeting was to remain secret. Still on an operational security basis, I was not to see my friends again and not to give anybody any news about myself. This was especially true for my family. Everybody was to ignore what had become of me. For this reason, I was not to return to the flat where I had spent the last few days and I was transferred to another flat. I was on my own and I was not to leave the flat. My personal belongings were brought to me from the previous flat and I did not see my friends from the 2e RSA again; I supposed they had failed selection and had been returned to their unit. I quickly received a new identity card by the name of Alain Wallon and I was told to destroy all my previous ID papers. While waiting to go to the UK, I tried to get used to my new name but it felt strange. I still was not used to it. Later on, I changed names on several other occasions and it then felt perfectly normal and never bothered me in the least"*

Except for a few details, this is the process each Sussex volunteer went through.

"Rémy" and "Saint-Jacques" went through all the personal files of the volunteers. Their work was not made any easier by the commanding officers of the volunteers' units who always were loath to lose good men; as early as the Summer of 1943, the two officers faced considerable difficulties to trace the right candidates but nevertheless, in February 1944, their task was completed and 120 servicemen were sent to the United Kingdom. Of course, the parent units of those men were not given any details of the whereabouts of their former soldiers. After a lengthy sea trip from Algiers or Casablanca made dangerous by attacks of German submarines, some of the volunteers finally arrived in London. Others flew directly from Maison Blanche (Algiers airport), had a stop-over in Casablanca, took off again in the evening and made a wide circle to the North in order to avoid the Portuguese, Spanish, French and British coasts before finally landing the next morning around 8 AM in Prestwick, in the North of Scotland.

On arriving in London, they had to go through another series of tests, exams and interrogations, they changed name once again and were made to write their will. Housed in the Free French volunteers' house in

Pembroke Lodge, not far from High Street Kensington, some of the future agents also got acquainted with their first Luftwaffe night bombing raids.

Once the administrative part was completed,

the volunteers were taken to Saint Albans, a small town located 40 km North of London. The MI 6 and OSS schools were there. A splendid British-style cottage by the name of "Praewood House", code-named "TS 7", housed the MI6 school. Its remoteness made it ideal for the operational security needs of a secret service. The newcomers dressed in British uniforms and after having changed name once again, were welcomed by Colonel Malcolm Henderson, commanding officer of the training centre.

In Saint Albans, which was surrounded by a large estate, the Military Police was in charge of area security. The inside of the building was quite grandiose, in the Victorian style. Another manor had been commandeered for this operation; it was located only a few hundred metres from there and was named Praewood House. For the duration of their training, the agents would go back and forth between those two buildings, either to follow classes or when off duty as they were accommodated on-site. All the Sussex agents went through those schools, their stay being comprised between four and six months depending on their arrival date.

*Opposite.*
**Reverse of an agent's marching order. The bearer of this order was sent from Algiers to St Albans in March 1944 in order to follow a training course.**
*(Sussex picture collection)*

# TRAINING

*Above.*
**Sussex agents being taught how to handle Harley Davidson and Matchless motorbikes in April 1944 in Banbury.**
*(Guy Wingate-collection Sussex picture)*

TRAINING was the responsibility of the authoritarian but highly respected Captain Guy Wingate who had been seconded as a mentor to the French agents.

In Praewood, apart from meal times and evenings, time was solely dedicated to technical and physical training. Classes covered all the topics necessary for an agent deployed in the field to successfully complete his mission. The organisation of the German armed forces was studied in depth with a specific emphasis placed on SS Panzer divisions such as the "Das Reich" and the "Hitlerjugend", as well as the Wehrmacht's "Panzer Lehr". The agents also had to be capable of recognising a Pzkw V Panther from a Pzkw VI Tiger. The way tank units were organized, the types of field artillery guns, the top speed of the different armoured vehicles,

*Opposite.*
**First page of Georges Soulier's training course notebook.**
*(Sussex picture collection)*

their weight, main armament, range, etc. all had to be mastered and specific exams ensured that the agents knew their lessons. Physical Training cessions were intense; they were led by British Commando physical training instructors and by two US Marines named Robichaud and O'Mola. *"The two instructors were good comrades for us as well as good teachers.... but it was sometimes painful. [...] Every morning, we had hand to hand combat cessions in order to be able to respond to an attack but also to be able to get a noiseless "clean kill" using only our hands to break the neck of our victim."*

American Lieutenant Vinciguerra was the shooting instructor. All kinds of weapons were used: pistols in several calibres, submachine guns, rifles, etc. German weapons were also used for those tactical shooting cessions so we would be able to operate with them. Just in case…

Driving lessons were also part of the training. We practised on trucks, buses and motorbikes (Harley Davidson, Matchless or Norton) since not many people knew how to ride those at the time etc. All those classes were extremely condensed and fast. Sabotage was of course one of the important topics and we handled all sort of explosives, grenades and booby traps.

Sometimes, the instructors organised boxing matches; two students were designated and sometimes amateur boxers were confronted to complete beginners. Weight, height and experience played little role in the choice of the instructors. Later, the agents understood that the instructors did not organise such matches for the fun of it or to see how well they could box; the idea was to evaluate the fighting spirit of the future agents. Obviously, if somebody was to "pack it in" on the boxing ring in front of a single man with boxing gloves, he would cave in during any brutal interrogation by German security personnel or Vichy miliciens with clubs, whips or even worst. Some of the candidates were "returned to unit" from Saint Albans

*Opposite.*
**OSS Lieutenant Douglas Alden a.k.a "Monsieur Martin", an instructor in St Albans**
*(Sussex picture collection)*

*Below.*
**A cartoon drawn by Lieutenant Kennedy depicting slightly mischievous Sussex "pupils" during a communication class in St Albans. The poster above the blackboard reads: "those who intend to work are requested not to bother those who don't do a thing!".**
*(Collection Sussex)*

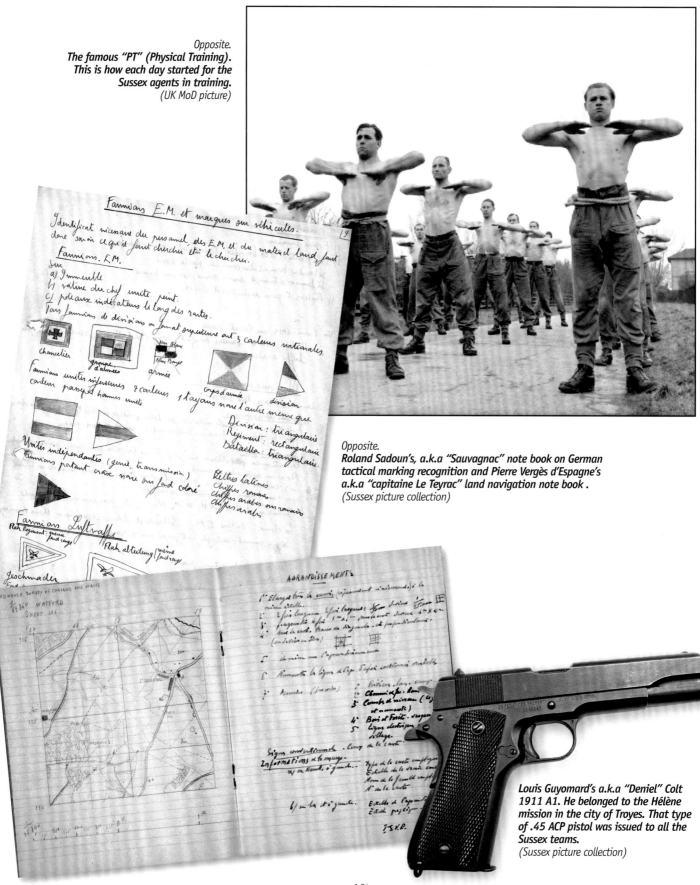

*Opposite.*
**The famous "PT" (Physical Training).**
**This is how each day started for the**
**Sussex agents in training.**
*(UK MoD picture)*

*Opposite.*
**Roland Sadoun's, a.k.a "Sauvagnac" note book on German**
**tactical marking recognition and Pierre Vergès d'Espagne's**
**a.k.a "capitaine Le Teyrac" land navigation note book .**
*(Sussex picture collection)*

**Louis Guyomard's a.k.a "Deniel" Colt**
**1911 A1. He belonged to the Hélène**
**mission in the city of Troyes. That type**
**of .45 ACP pistol was issued to all the**
**Sussex teams.**
*(Sussex picture collection)*

because they lacked the required aggressiveness.

Land navigation was also part of the sylla-bus. It was crucial that the agent could send the right coordinates for dropping or landing zones or that he could mark a landing strip in the required manner for a pick-up operation. Night navigation exercises were common; the students were dropped by truck in an unknown location somewhere in the British countryside and they were told to make for a given point and to reach it in a given time. The exercise was made more difficult by the fact that all the road signs and milestones had been removed in 1940 in anticipation of a German landing. Night navigation exercises had to be scrupu-lously well prepared and standard operating procedures had to be respected. Smoking and talking was prohibited and map reading with a torch was only done under the cover of a coat just like it was supposed to be done when deployed on operations.

The radio operators spent days after days learning how to code and decode messages.

*"Several systems were in use but the most com-mon was the double transposition cypher. Sche-matically, with this system, you had to write the message on a piece of paper with small squares, each letter being separated from the next; there were no interval between the words. They were then re-written a second time but horizontally, but reading the first message vertically; finally, the operation was to be done a third time.*

*To make things just a bit more complicated, vertical columns were not read from left to right one after the other but they were read in a dis-persed order. This order was given by words that were extracted from a poem that each agent chose but which remained the same for the duration of the mission.*

On top of that training, the radio operators were of course trained on the different sets they would use on operation. Setting the aerial

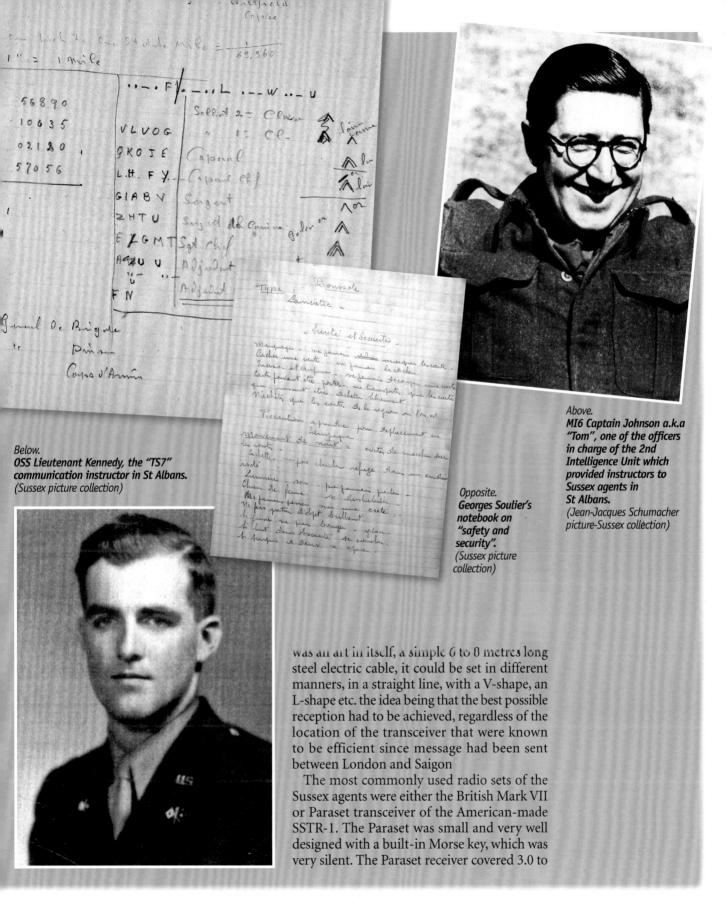

$1'' = 1 \text{ mile}$

Below.
**OSS Lieutenant Kennedy, the "TS7" communication instructor in St Albans.**
(Sussex picture collection)

Above.
**MI6 Captain Johnson a.k.a "Tom", one of the officers in charge of the 2nd Intelligence Unit which provided instructors to Sussex agents in St Albans.**
(Jean-Jacques Schumacher picture-Sussex collection)

Opposite.
**Georges Soulier's notebook on "safety and security".**
(Sussex picture collection)

was an art in itself, a simple 6 to 8 metres long steel electric cable, it could be set in different manners, in a straight line, with a V-shape, an L-shape etc. the idea being that the best possible reception had to be achieved, regardless of the location of the transceiver that were known to be efficient since message had been sent between London and Saigon

The most commonly used radio sets of the Sussex agents were either the British Mark VII or Paraset transceiver of the American-made SSTR-1. The Paraset was small and very well designed with a built-in Morse key, which was very silent. The Paraset receiver covered 3.0 to

*Opposite.*
OSS Major Justin O'Brien who was in charge of
the organization of both Sussex and Proust missions. This picture
was dedicated to madame Andrée Goubillon, the "Mummy"
of the Sussex agents and owner of the café Sussex.
*(Sussex picture collection)*

*Above.*
**Captain Guy Wingate of the Intelligence Corps. He was tasked
with the training of Sussex agents. He took part in the liberation
of Paris alongside Sussex teams in August 1944.**
*(Sussex picture collection)*

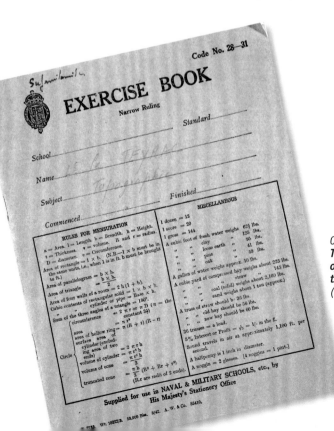

*Opposite.*
**Guy Wingate's intelligence
Corps Insigna.**
*(Sussex picture collection)*

*Opposite.*
**The first page of one
of capitaine Le Teyrac's
training notebooks.**
*(Sussex picture collection)*

7.6 MHz in one band while the transmitter covered 3.3 to 4.5 MHz and 4.5 to 7.6 MHz in two bands, selectable by a toggle switch. The gain of the antenna was 4 to 5 watts. The SSTR-1 was heavier but also more powerful. These two sets could fit in an ordinary looking suitcase and could only broadcast messages in Morse code. Two other sets were used to listen to BBC broadcasts, the British MCR-1 also called the "Biscuit" and the American Emerson set. Both operated on batteries so that the agent could still listen to the broadcasts when the main was cut, a frequent occurrence at the time. Finally, and mostly after the 6 June landings, some teams were equipped with the S-Phone system, an ultra high frequency duplex radio telephone system which was used for ground to air communications. A specific B25 Mitchell squadron, placed under the command of Squadron Leader Whinney was created in order to support Sussex missions that used the S-Phone. This squadron received a number of Free French airmen on secondment including famous writer Joseph Kessel and his friend André Bernheim. Their role was to establish contact with the French speaking Sussex missions operating on the grounds so that they could act as forward air control parties in support of allied artillery and close air support against enemy troop concentrations.

The training syllabus was very comprehensive and all aspects of clandestine warfare were studied; nevertheless, when the agent had finished these courses, there was another hurdle!

*Opposite.*
**Crossing the Thames near Windsor. In the foreground, a British Army Lance-Corporal seconded to the Sussex plan as an instructor. Georges Ducasse a.k.a "Chaloner" can be identified squatting near the stern.**
*(Guy Wingate picture/ Sussex collection.)*

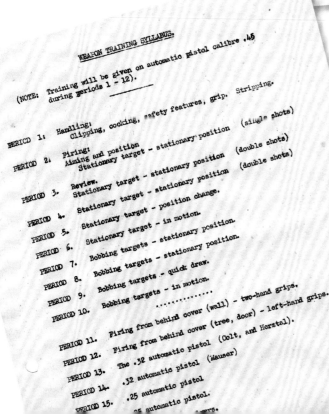

# CLOSE COMBAT SYLLABUS.

**Period 1.** Introduction.
Demonstration of efficiency of the Method.
Basic blows
  a)  edge of the hand
  b)  chin jab
  c)  side kick (one foot)
  d)  flying jump (both feet)
  e)  knee

**Period 2.** Review.
Breaking wrist and throat holds (one hand and two hands)
Breaking hair hold.

**Period 3.** Review.
Breaking Front Bear Hug (over and under arms)
Alternative over-arm release.

**Period 4.** Review.
Breaking Rear Bear Hug (over and under arms)
Alternative over-arm release.

**Period 5.** Review.
Application of thumb hold and sentry hold.
Japanese stranglehold.

**Period 6.** Handcuff hold.
Bent arm hold.
Head hold.
Review.

..................

**Period 7.** Review.
Throws (hip, wrist, back)
Matchbox attack
Newspaper attack
Double ear

**Period 8.** Review.
Getting 
Break-aw

**Period 9.** Review.
Stick 
How to

**Period 10.** Revi
Use

**Period 11.** Dis

**Period 12.** F

---

## ALLOCATION OF SUBJECTS.

| SUBJECT | | INSTRUCTOR |
|---|---|---|
| MAP READING AND SKETCHING | ........ | (1) Lt. BYFIELD |
| | | (2) Lt. WINGATE |
| WEAPON TRAINING | ............. | (3) Sq. Ldr. ZIEGLER |
| | | (1) Lt. WINGATE |
| CLOSE COMBAT | ......... | (2) Sgt. ROBICHAUD |
| | | (3) Sgt. HOMOLA |
| MOTOR CYCLING | ....... | (1) Sgt. ROBICHAUD |
| | | (2) Sgt. HOMOLA |
| | | (3) Lt. WATSON. |
| FIRST AID | ........ | (1) Capt. JOHNSON |
| | | (2) Lt. WINGATE |
| | | (3) Sgt. McDAIN. |
| OBSTACLE COURSE | ........ | (1) Lt. WATSON |
| | | (2) Lt. BYFIELD |
| ...ARY | .......... | (1) Sgt. ROBICHAUD |
| | | (2) Sgt. HOMOLA |
| | .......... | (1) Capt. JOHNSON |
| | | (2) Lt. WATSON |
| | | (3) Capt. PATON |
| | | (4) Lt. BYFIELD. |
| ...General | .......... | (1) Capt. PATON |
| | | (2) Sq. Ldr. ZIEGLER |
| | | (3) Lt. MACY |
| ...al | .......... | (1) Lt. MACY |
| | | (2) Lt. WATSON |
| | | (3) Major KEYSER. |
| | .......... | (1) Lt. WATSON |
| | | (2) Lt. MACY |
| | | (3) Major KEYSER |
| | | (1) Capt. EMERY |
| | | (2) Sgt. BIRDSALL |

20. 11. 43

---

## WEAPON TRAINING SYLLABUS.

(NOTE: Training will be given on automatic pistol calibre .45
during Periods 1 - 12).

**PERIOD 1:** Handling:
Clipping, cocking, safety features, grip. Stripping.

**PERIOD 2:** Firing:
Aiming and position
Stationary target - stationary position (single shots)

**PERIOD 3.** Review.
Stationary target - stationary position (double shots)

**PERIOD 4.** Stationary target - stationary position (double shots)

**PERIOD 5.** Stationary target - position change.

**PERIOD 6.** Stationary target - in motion.

**PERIOD 7.** Bobbing targets - stationary position.

**PERIOD 8.** Bobbing targets - stationary position.

**PERIOD 9.** Bobbing targets - quick draw.

**PERIOD 10.** Bobbing targets - in motion.

..............

**PERIOD 11.** Firing from behind cover (wall) - two-hand grips.

**PERIOD 12.** Firing from behind cover (tree, door) - left-hand grips.

**PERIOD 13.** The .32 automatic pistol (Colt, and Herztal).

**PERIOD 14.** .32 automatic pistol (Mauser)

**PERIOD 15.** .25 automatic pistol

.25 automatic pistol

---

*Opposite.*
*Three pages from the secret Sussex training syllabus with the names of all the instructors as well as a list of the different subject matters taught to the agents: close combat, weapon training, map reading and sketching, enemy equipment and uniforms recognition, etc.). Nine copies of that specific document were produced.*
*(Sussex picture collection)*

*Left page*
*In the Glenalmond gardens, left to right: Zuber, X, Guy Wingate's clerk, Guy Wingate and Julien Fayet.*
*(Guy Wingate picture/ Sussex collection.)*

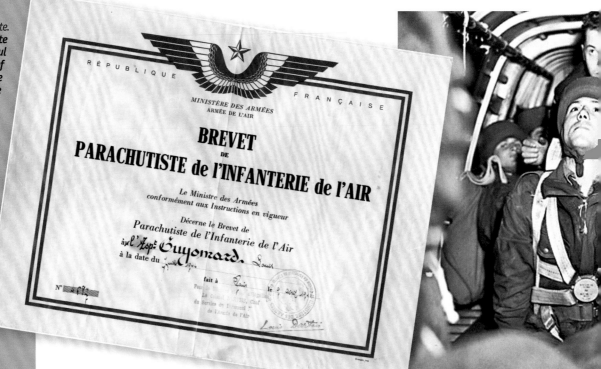

# THE PARACHUTE COURSE

Agent Sussex followed an accelerated, one-week parachute course at the famous British parachute school located at Ringway near Manchester. Georges Soulier remembers:

*"After two or three months of courses, I was sent to Manchester in order to follow the parachute course. At this time, the parachute course was a long-winded affair and the first jump was only performed after several weeks. But for us, things were to be different! We left on a Sunday evening by train for Manchester. An old British officer whom I did not know but who had a distinct "British Indian army" look about him came along with us. As soon as we arrived on Monday morning, we started doing physical training cessions like there was no tomorrow and we were taught all about the different "parachute landing falls"; we were told that when we hit the ground, we were not to try to remain standing but instead we had to bend our legs and roll to the ground so as not to end up with a fractured limb. Then, we jumped from a plane mock-up; in the afternoon, we did the same*

*Opposite.*
**During the parachute course in Ringway, an exercise to learn how to collapse the parachute canopy once on the ground and learning how to jump through the "Joe hole".**
*(UK MoD picture)*

*Parachute training in Ringway: for the Sussex trainee agents, this accelerated course only lasted about a week. It concluded with a series of jumps first from a balloon and then from an aircraft, the last descent being completed at night. The agent was only considered as "badged" once he or she had done an operational jump.*
(UK MoD picture)

*Free French airborne wings belonging to Louis Guyomard. This is the bullion version with a "Bleu Louise" French air force uniform backing.*
(Photo collection Sussex)

exercises but we were made to jump from the fourth floor of a house. Just outside the window of the fourth floor, a wooden platform had been jury-rigged; it had a one-metre wide circular hole in its middle. A steel cable was attached to a big pulley fitted with winglets. When the cable unfurled, as it picked up speed, the winglets would gradually slow the cable down. Straps were fitted to the cable; we hooked ourselves to them and then sat on the verge of the hole. The para jump instructor (PJI) then shouted "Action station"; you were expected to seat up straight and be ready; then, he shouted "Go" and you had to launch yourself in the empty hole. The fall was fast but the winglet slowed us down enough and nobody was injured on landing. This was a bit frightening, probably even a bit more than jumping from a real plane. We had to do this exercise several times.

On Tuesday morning, we were subjected to the same

regime and then, at the end of the day, we were taken to the airfield. A para jump instructor showed us what an open parachute looked like, how to fold it when on the ground and how to don it. Then, he boarded a Whitley bomber, which flew over the airfield and he jumped right over us, landing gently, near us. We heard later that on a subsequent parachute course, he did the same demonstration but his parachute did a roman candle and he crashed in front of his pupils! This caused them a bit of an understandable shock. After his demonstration, the para jump instructor invited us to do just like him. Nowadays, jumping with a parachute is a fairly benign activity but back then it was not and I cannot say we were brimming with confidence as we boarded the plane and even less when the para jump instructor opened the circular hole in the floor of the bomber through which we could see the countryside speeding away beneath us. After having hooked the static line, which would soon pull the parachute from its bag to a cable, I sat on the verge of the hole. My heart was beating fast and a red light started shining above the door. Then, the PJI shouted

the customary "Action station". Almost immediately, the light above the door switched to green; the PJI then shouted "Go !" even louder. It felt like the crack of a whip! I threw myself into the hole without thinking twice.

I felt a strong jolt almost immediately. My parachute had just opened and the feeling was tremendous. After the din of the engines, it was eerily quiet; I was going down gently and I was feeling fine. I did a textbook landing, just as I had been told. On Wednesday, we were taught how to fold a parachute and in the afternoon I did a second jump; on Thursday, I did a third jump and on Friday morning a fourth. Then it was the time for the mandatory night jump. This jump was done from a tethered balloon; linked to a truck by a cable, it went up to three hundred metres and it could be brought up or down at will. The wicker basket had a hole on its middle, just like the Withley. When I jumped, I initially thought that my parachute had failed to open. This was due to the lack of horizontal speed of the tethered balloon, which meant that the straps and risers of the parachute took longer to deploy; I hissed a sigh of relief when it finally did and hit the ground almost immediately, once again without any injury.

Our parachute training was thus over; it had lasted only five days!

On Saturday, after having toasted our success, we returned to Saint Albans. We would only be awarded our wings after having performed an operational jump. Our training phase was almost over. Now we had to put theory into practise during a culmination exercise, which was designed to recreate the conditions we would face during our future mission in occupied France."

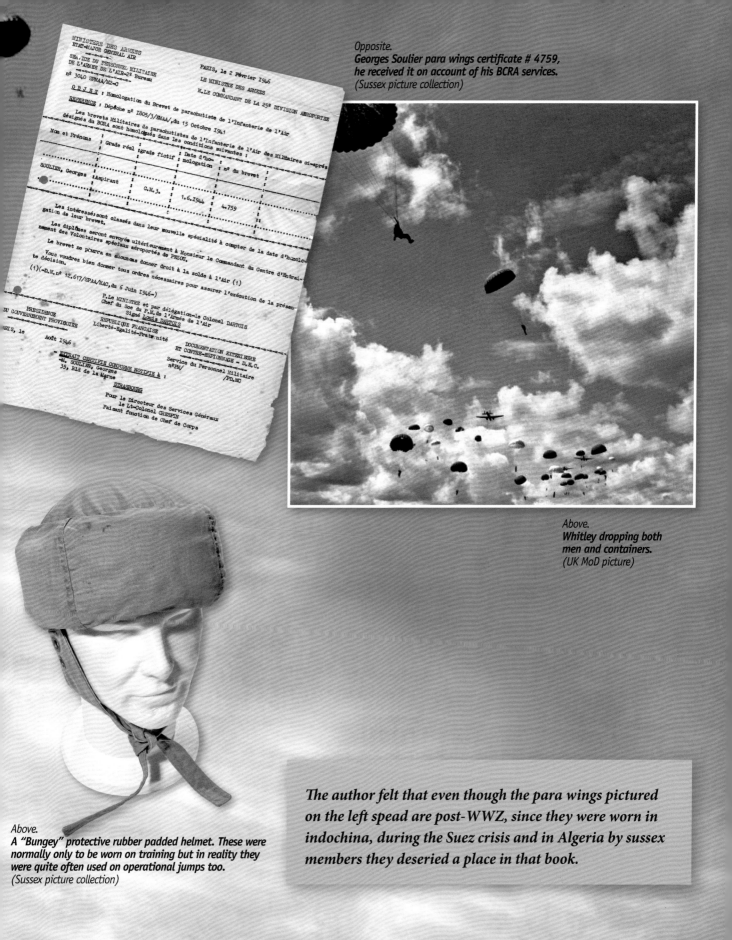

MINISTERE DES ARMEES
ETAT-MAJOR GENERAL AIR

SERVICE DU PERSONNEL MILITAIRE
DE L'ARMEE DE L'AIR-2e Bureau
n° 3040 SPMAA/MZ-Q

PARIS, le 2 Février 1946

LE MINISTRE DES ARMEES
à
M.LE COMMANDANT DE LA 25e DIVISION AEROPORTEE

OBJET : Homologation du Brevet de parachutiste de l'Infanterie de l'Air

REFERENCE : Dépêche n° 1805/3/SMAA/,du 15 Octobre 1941

Les brevets Militaires de parachutistes de l'Infanterie de l'Air des Militaires ci-après
désignés du BCRA sont homologués dans les conditions suivantes :

| Nom et Prénoms | Grade réel | grade fictif | Date d'homologation | n° du brevet |
|---|---|---|---|---|
| SOULIER, Georges | Aspirant | C.M.3. | 1.6.1944 | 4.759 |

Les intéressés sont classés dans leur nouvelle spécialité à compter de la date d'homologation de leur brevet.

Les diplômes seront envoyés ultérieurement à Monsieur le Commandant du Centre d'Entrainement des Volontaires spéciaux aéroportés de PEZOU.

Le brevet ne pourra en aucunes donner droit à la solde à l'Air (1)

Vous voudrez bien donner tous ordres nécessaires pour assurer l'exécution de la présente décision.

(1)(-D.M. n° 12.617/SPAA/MAC,du 6 Juin 1946-)

P.Le MINISTRE et par délégation-le Colonel DARTOIS
Chef du Soc du P.M.de l'Armée de l'Air
Signé Louis DARTOIS

PRESIDENCE
DU GOUVERNEMENT PROVISOIRE

REPUBLIQUE FRANCAISE
Liberté-Egalité-Fraternité

PARIS, le        Août 1946

DOCUMENTATION EXTERIEURE
ET CONTRE-ESPIONNAGE - D.E.C.
Service du Personnel Militaire
n°PM/                /PD,MC

EXTRAIT CERTIFIE CONFORME NOTIFIE A :
-M. SOULIER, Georges
35, Bld de la Marne
STRASBOURG

Pour le Directeur des Services Généraux
le Lt-Colonel CRESPIN
Faisant fonction de Chef de Corps

*Opposite.*
**Georges Soulier para wings certificate # 4759,
he received it on account of his BCRA services.**
*(Sussex picture collection)*

*Above.*
**Whitley dropping both
men and containers.**
*(UK MoD picture)*

*Above.*
**A "Bungey" protective rubber padded helmet. These were
normally only to be worn on training but in reality they
were quite often used on operational jumps too.**
*(Sussex picture collection)*

*The author felt that even though the para wings pictured
on the left spead are post-WWZ, since they were worn in
indochina, during the Suez crisis and in Algeria by sussex
members they deseried a place in that book.*

# EXERCICE « FANNY »

T*HIS CULMINATION EXERCISE was the end of the training phase. Its aim was to develop survival behaviours for the agents who would soon have to operate covertly in a hostile environment. At the end of the exercise, "as if by mistake" the agents were arrested by the police and subjected to intense questioning in conditions that tried to mirror reality as much as possible. This was a way to prepare them for the mental rigours that some of them would soon encounter.*

*Georges Soulier takes up the story:*
*"This four or five-day exercise took place in Stratford-on-Avon, Shakespeare's native town. Stratford was a small town of about 20,000 souls located south of Birmingham. I had taken lodging with a local police commander who knew about my situation but who had to keep silent about it as the police played the opposing force in our exercise.*

*The aim of this activity was to practise all I had learnt on tailing, contacts, etc. but also and mostly it*

*was meant for me to get caught and see how I would conduct myself after capture in the hands of policemen who really thought they held an enemy agent. This was also suppose to provide me with some "real" experience as the local police had been warned about the presence of French agents operating on behalf of the Germans. Each day, the police would receive additional information on our whereabouts, which meant that the noose was being slowly tightened on us. Each day, I had a contact with my teammate in a different place within the town, as we did not lodge in the same area. We had different signs to indicate if we were being tailed. If we had a tail, we had to stop and tie our shoelace; if we weren't, we would lit up a cigarette. The first four days went well. On the fifth, my teammate called me on the phone to give me a rendezvous at 1300 hours in front of Christ Church, a church located on one end of Main Street with many streets leading into it. I made for the rendezvous with enough time to spare and checked for any indication of a tail; the street in which I lived was empty, as usual. The only presence was a worker in a boiler suit with a toolbox on a sling riding a bicycle towards me; he seemed oblivious to my presence.*

*As I reached Main Street, there was a bit more people but nothing seemed to be out of its place; it was the same when I reached the square in Christ Church. The only problem was that I could not see my teammate; I then thought that maybe he was hiding while waiting for me so I lit up a cigarette. As I did that, I noticed the worker in his boiler suit that I had previously seen in my street; without a doubt, he was watching me. Then, cars appeared from the different streets and started closing in on me at low speed. Understanding that something was happening, I tried to look unimpressed and started walking away from the square at a leisurely pace. It was too late; policemen in plain cloth jumped out of several cars, came up to me and ordered me to follow them; I had no choice but to obey. They took me to the town's police station and showed me into a room on the first floor of the building. Immediately, after having emptied my pockets and analysed what they held, they started interrogating me.*

*I had to confess my name (the alias, of course), explain when I arrived in the UK, how I got there and why; the reasons of my presence in Stratford, etc. I had prepared some answers in anticipation of those* moments but in order to limit the risks of confusing myself, I had created a story by which I only had arrived in the UK three weeks ago; my reason for being in Stratford being of course my admiration for the famous poet and my wish to know his birthplace.

The questioning lasted for nearly six hours, until 1900 hours. The police inspectors were always very well behaved and they offered me some tea at 1700 hours.

During a pause, we discussed about things and others, including music. I thought that I was home safe and that I did not risk blowing my own cover. We talked about a musician who then was very famous in London and who had done a memorable concert in the Royal Albert Hall. I had seen that concert and I mentioned it without giving it a second thought. Then, the questioning took a new turn. From my "pocket litter", the policemen produced a rolled piece of paper, a piece of the programme handed over during that famous concert. The inspectors told me that this show had taken place more than a month before the date I was supposed to have arrived in the UK. I was of course trapped; I tried to get away with a few unconvincing explanations. It was then 1900 hours and the inspectors told me they would start everything all over again and that I had now better tell the truth. I knew I had to quickly find something to get out of this situation. Right at this moment, the door of the interrogation room flew open and the chief constable walked in with Captain Saint Clair; my saviour had arrived. All along, from the room next door, they had been listening in to the interrogation thanks to a microphone. In front of the bewildered inspectors, with a big smile, he came to shake my hand and told me the exercise was now over and that I had not done too badly. The police inspectors who by then thought they had caught some big fish were of course disappointed but they were good sports and they all shook my hand. This episode had taught me a lesson and in future missions I always checked the content of my pockets thoroughly. After this final test, I returned to Saint Albans. My training days were over.

William Bechtel, another agent under training, was supposed to send intelligence reports to Saint Albans on American and British military exercises that were taking place between Nottingham and Leicester.

William had found lodging with the commander of the local "Home Guard". This person did not ask any question when Bechtel settled in his first floor room and their daily exchanges were perfectly normal. Nevertheless, the lodger was quite surprised when William stubbornly refused to give his dirty washing to his wife; William said he was very particular about

his laundry and that he preferred to wash it himself so the lodger did not insist. At the end of the first day, William washed his shirt and a few handkerchief; before the owner of the house even had time to offer his dryer, William had strung a piece of wire to which he hung his washing. Of course, this washing line was the aerial of his radio. Every evening, he went to the pub where the officers who took part in the exercise used to end the day. On his first visit, a group of field-grade officers asked him if he wanted to join them. The presence of this fifty-something French officer who had fought during the battle of Bir-Hacheim was a source of amusement for two British Colonels. On every occasion, the exercises of the day were commented but William did not seem overly interested by their conversation. Several times, the British officers asked William what a French officer would have done in their position; he invariably answered with the most

*Above and below.*
**Different views of Straford-upon-Avon where many a Sussex "Fanny" exercise took place.**
(A. Milton picture)

Above.
**The Home Guard and police could always be counted on to play "enemy" during the final Sussex exercises.**
(Jon Mills picture)

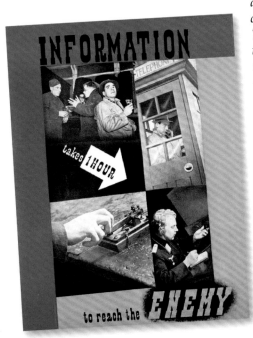

attitude of the British officers was probably linked to what was happening on the main square, which looked more and more like the preparation of a military parade. Considering these combined exercises had already attracted a lot of general officers, this parade could only mean that a very important personality was probably about to arrive in the area...

So, beer in hand, William left the bar and went straight to the British officers; with a quiet voice, as if sharing a secret, he asked them: "Is he coming alone?"

The question of the Frenchman seemed to relieve the two British officers and their faces suddenly lit up; one of the two Colonels, looking fairly reassured told William:

- "So you knew Montgomery was coming tomorrow at 08.00 AM?"

- "Of course" answered William quietly.

From then on, the two officers opened up; they were tasked with the security of the Field Marshal and they felt they had not been given enough men for the job. In order to make them feel better, William pretended he once had to carry out a fairly similar mission as the Afrika Korps was supposedly drawing near... William had recovered the trust of the two officers who left the pub earlier than normal because they still had a lot of details to sort out before the next day. William quickly returned to his room and sent his intelligence report to Saint Albans. Once this was done, he spared a thought for the two officers, thinking their careless talks would probably affect their careers negatively. Earlier than normal, the next day, Bechtel went out to buy the papers before returning to his lodging for breakfast. He had not walked 100 metres when a car stopped at his level; he heard a door opening and then a familiar voice told him:

- Get in Bechtel!

- Colonel Henderson! said William who, for a moment, had been taken aback.

As soon as got into the black limousine, he noticed that somebody was seating next to Colonel Henderson. The CO of Saint Albans school showed a lot of respect to this mysterious man dressed in civilian clothes. Sat between the two, William was not feeling quite right. The car having started again, Henderson told William:

- Pray tell me right now the name of the person who gave you the details of Monty's arrival!

As William remained silent, Henderson said:

- This secret was only known by six field grade officers; William, I want names, and sharpish!

In a second, William understood what he had started; he smiled and looked at Henderson who appeared to be extremely embarrassed.

- Sir, you taught us never to give away our sources!

far-fetched solutions, triggering roars of laughter. Once the happy officers had left the pub, William returned to his bedroom and reported the details of the day's military operations he had gathered.

The next evening, William's attention was drawn to a group of soldiers who were drawing lines on the main square of Melton-Mowbray. As usual, he sat at the bar and waited for the officers he had engaged with previously. They arrived later than usual, looking tense, and this time, they did not invite him at their table and spoke with hushed voices. This behaviour alarmed William who first thought he had been identified and that his main source of intelligence was no longer accessible. He then analysed that it was unlikely that his cover was blown because any sensible intelligence service would have encouraged the two colonels to keep on meeting him for counter intelligence purpose. The worries of the two Colonels had nothing to do with him.

William then thought that the

*Opposite.*
**A Home Guard Sergent in an ambush position during an exercise against "enemy agents".**
(Jon Mills picture)

- William, that is enough, uttered the Colonel who showed signs of losing patience.

The conversation lasted for several minutes; the driver looked repeatedly in his rear-view mirror as he seemed a bit worried at the turn of events while Colonel Henderson did not know how to cope with William's attitude and silence.

Having remained silent from the beginning of the conversation, the mysterious character in civilian clothes suddenly spoke.

- I want your word that your source of information does not present a threat to operational security….

- You have my word said William with relief.

- ENDEX  said Henderson sighing heavily.

All the Sussex teams had to go through such exercises that were all named "Fanny"! Now, all they had left to do was to get ready for their operational missions.

Captain Douglas Alden one of the OSS Sussex instructors in Saint Alban recalled:

Living with these young men who all seemed so courageous and idealistic when they were joking and telling stories about their training exercises was one of my life's most enriching experience. Our dining room was separated from the GI's eating facilities and we often received visitors from the BCRA. Those parachutists came from all walks of life; some had a rural background, others stemmed from the nobility, as I was to learn after the liberation. All those young Frenchmen wore the British battle dress with the rank of Lieutenant. Among the oldest in the group were Major Marcel Saubestre as well as two Captains, William Bechtel and Pierre Vergès d'Espagne a.k.a "Le Teyrac". The ambiance was really good and I still can remember this anecdote. One day, a rumour was spreading saying that General Donovan was soon going to inspect us. The GIs then started having fun by calling "Attention" every other minute. Of course, when General Donovan arrived for good, nobody paid any attention to the order. On that day, the whole top floor was a mess because the agents were sorting out their kit.

Finally, I will never forget the excitement of the first operational departure. With the help of a US Marine Sergeant, our teams started packing their own containers with equipment and supplies including a number of British copies of typically Gallic items such as Gauloises cigarettes. They were provided by the British secret services. We also gave them huge sums of genuine French banknotes. Every time we went to Harrington airfield with a team, the OSS motor pool in London would send us a British car with American drivers. Justin O'Brien was such a maniac about operational security that on the first mission we did not use the drivers and we took the wheel instead. The first mission was on!

*Opposite.*
**Home Guard units training in urban operations.**
(Jon Mills picture)

Opposite.
**The complete kit list of sussex agents :**
**clothingtoiletries, weapons, documents,**
**radio equipements, etc.**
*(Sussex photo collection)*

LISTE D'EQUIPEMENT DE ....................

Documents: (Obligatoires)

Carte d'Identite
Carte de revitaillement
Carte de textile
Papiers de demobilisation
Certificat de Recensement
Certificat de Travail

Documents: (Auxiliaires)

Permis de conduire
Carte de Jeunesse Francaise
Carte d'etudiant

Argent

....................francs

Vetements en sac de voyage

1 costume usage
2 chemises
1 cravate
2 paires de chaussettes
1 paire de souliers
1 camisole
2 calecons
3 mouchoirs

Vetements portes par l'agent

1 chapeau, beret ou casquette
1 costume
1 chemise
1 cravate
1 paire de chaussettes
1 paire de souliers
1 camisole
1 calecon
1 ceinture
1 mouchoir
1 manteau ou impermeable
1 paire de gants
1 echarpe
1 pullover
1 ceinture argent

Articles de toilette en sac

1 Rasoir francais (manche e
10 lames de rechange
1 blaireau (manche evide)
2 savons pour la barbe
6 morceaux de savon
2 essuie mains
1 miroir et peigne
1 paquet d'epingles a s
1 brosse a dents
1 tube de pate dentifri

Trousse Medicale

British brown kit (SC
1 paquent a pansement

Nourriture et tabac

1 ration pour 24 heures
1 ration pour 48 heures
8 tablettes de chocolat francais
1 paquet de pillules stimulantes
1 rechaud meta
65 paquets de cigarettes francaises
6 boites d'alumettes francaises
41 paquets de saccharine
7 livres de cafe
2 petits sacs de tabac
1 kg savon de Marseilles

Armes

1 revolver calibre .32
50 balles
1 couteau de commando
1 stylo lance gaz lacrimogene
2 grenades, type 69 ou 36

Cartes et Instruments

1 Boussole (lensatic)
1 regle (centimetres)
1 couteau de poche
1 loupe
2 crayons, rouge et bleu
1 gomme
1 bloc de papier a ecrire
1 stylo

1 a 4 cartes de la regoin GSGS 1:50,000
4 reductions photographiques des cartes des regions adjacentes 1:100,000
1 plan de la ville
1 carte Michelin de la region - edition francaise
1 carte Michelin de la region - edition anglaise

Divers

2 blocs de papier QB
1 gourde de cognac
1 trousse de reparation bicyclette
1 bague ou un bouton de col boussole
1 lampe de poche
1 ampoules de rechange
3 piles de rechange
1 lampe electrique Americaine pour signaux. Lentille mica(couleur verte).
1 couteau d'evasion a plusieurs lames
1 lime d'evasion
1 montre bracelet Suisse
1 paquet de pillules L
1 paquet de pillules K
1 portefeuille
2 enveloppe de bicyclette
1 necessaire de reparation
2 paires de lacets

Observateur seulement

1 telescope de poche
1 bague en or evidee
1 crayon evide

Ascension

1 Emetteur
1 recepteur
1 accumulateur de secours (Willard)
1 rechargeur a main
3 bouteilles d'acide sulphurique.

Radios seulement
Radio et materiel

1 Emetteur et recepteur
    complets (TR1)
1 Emetteur et recepteur de
    secours (Mark 21)
1 accumulateur de secours (Willard)
3 bouteilles d'acide sulphurique
1 rechargeur a main
1 tableau de signaux
Codes

# SUSSEX missions lest

| N° badge & PSEUDO/AKA | | NOMS REELS / AKA NAMES | | DATE | LIEU DE PARACHUTAGE |
|---|---|---|---|---|---|
| 1 JEANNETTE | 4 MARCEL | GUYOT | SAUBESTRE | 08-09/02/1944 | Loches (Indre & Loire) |
| 2 LESCOUR (P) | 3 LUCIEN † | LASSALLE (P) | BINET † | | |
| 5 BECHTEL | 6 VALLADE | BECHTEL | VIARNAUD | 09-10/04/1944 | Ruffec-le-Château, 8 km E Le Blanc (Indre) |
| 7 CHAROT | 8 TRAL | BROCHART | LART | | |
| 9 CLAUZEL (P) | 10 COULON | MAUREL (P) | VERGON | | |
| 11 VOYER † | 12 LEBEAU | VOYER † | GUILLEBAUD | 10-11/04/1944 | Ruffec-le-Château, 8 km E Le Blanc (Indre) |
| 15 GUICHARD | 13 DUVALLET | DELHOMME | REVERET | | |
| 16 LEBEL | 14 GEAY | GUERRINI | DUCHATEAU | | |
| 19 BESSONE | 20 BEIGNET | DEGORSE | SCHOULER | 07-08/05/1944 | 5 km E Souppes-sur-Loing - DZ La Brosse (Seine et Marne) |
| 18 LAUGIER | 17 THIBERT | GUENARD | ANDREU | 07-08/05/1944 | 6 km N E St Oulph (Aube) |
| FONTANES | 47 ASNIER † | BERTRAND | ANCERGUES | 09-10/05/1944 | Nicorbin - 4 km N Voves (Eure et Loir) |
| 100 GOUDELIN † | 101 MARCHAND † | GUYOMARD C † | MILLET † | 10-11/05/1944 | NEAUFLES / RISLES (Eure) |
| 21 BERTRAND | 22 LAUNE | DE PERTHUIS | DRAN | | |
| 23 JOYEUSE | 24 CHALONER | VEUVE | DUCASSE | 28-29/05/1944 | Nicorbin - 4 km N Voves (Eure et Loir) |
| 25 PICOT (P) | 26 CAUMONT (P) | LACQUEMANT (P) | BECK (P) | | |
| 27 FRANCOIS (PNR) | 28 FOURNIERE (PNR) | ROUPAIN † | GIRBAL † | | |
| 33 JOURDET | 34 BOUDEMANGE | VAAS | SOULIER | 01-02/06/1944 | S Savennières, Rochefort/Loire (Maine et Loire) |
| 35 BOUCHOT | 36 BORDIER | HUMBERT | SAUTIERE | | |
| 31 MONTJEAN | 32 BOISSIER | BROCHARD | PEDRO | | |
| 29 LEDRON | 30 PIRON | LEFEVRE | POMERANZ | | |
| 37 CORBIN | 38 CREMIEUX | FAUROUX | BLANDIN | 06-07/06/1944 | Preuilly / Claise (Indre et Loire) |
| 39 VERNEUIL | 40 BOUSQUET† | PISSIER | TOSI | 07-08/06/1944 | E La Ferté Alais (Essonne) |
| 41 COLLARD | 42 OLLIVIER | LEROYER | COULON | 07-08/06/1944 | Villiers sous Grez (Seine et Marne) |
| 43 NEDELEC | 44 LEBLANC | QUENTEL | PASCO | 16-17/06/1944 | Maquis La Mouette - Saint-Marcel (Morbihan) |
| 51 KERGOUR | 52 DUJARDIN | DE BEAUCORPS | BARRE | | Château l'Hermitage (Sarthe) |
| 50 GIRARD † | | FOSSET † | | | |
| 48 DUTAL † | 49 MAURIN † | CROCQ † | BISCAINO † | 03-04/07/1944 | |
| 45 LAURENT | 46 FERRIERES † | RIGOT | NOËL † | | |
| | 59 CHAMONET † | | CLOPET † | 08-09/07/1944 | Averton (Mayenne) |
| 54 MARCHAND † | 53 THENET | MULLER † | REFANCHE | 05-06/07/1944 | S Fouilleuse, DZ Talon (Oise) |
| 55 PHILIPPE | 56 D'ARZAC | LINVINGSTONE | BURTEY | | |
| 63 CABOSSEL | 64 DIGNE | LEMAITRE | BRUNET | 07-08/07/1944 | N Bièvre, 6 km S Orbais l'Abbaye (Marne) |
| 62 GROSSOT | 65 CREPY | DE ROUX | MOUROCQ | | |
| 60 DUBOST | 61 DENIEL | BEAUREL | GUYOMARD | | |
| 66 NALBRUNEY | 67 BEON | QUILLENT | HERRY | | |
| 57 BLANC | 58 VERNEZ | DE SORBIER | RAVARRE | 08-09/07/1944 | Averton (Mayenne) |
| 68 SAGAN | 69 BERLIOZ | STRAUSS | BOQUET | 10-11/07/1944 | Saint-Caprais (Allier) |
| 76 GRELEUR | 77 COLIN | GUEDELOT | BERTIN | 20-21/07/1944 | 5 km E Souppes-sur-Loing DZ La Brosse (Seine et Marne) |
| 70 HENOCQUE | 71 AURY | FOLY | RADURON | | |
| 74 MARTIN (PNR) | 75 CORNU | MIGNONNEAU (PNR) | DELPLANQUE | | |
| 72 CARLIER | 73 DESMARCHAIS | R PORLIER | E GENDARME | | |
| 84 ADAM | 85 PAUTARD | AUBERGER | OESTERLE | 30-31/07/1944 | 5 km E Souppes-sur-Loing DZ La Brosse (Seine et Marne) |
| 78 ROUX | 79 PETITJEAN | POUX | GROSJEAN | | |
| 82 GARETTE | 83 BEAUFILS | CARILLON | PAUL | | |
| 81 MEYNIEL | 80 PIERLOT | LECOMTE | PRALONG | | |
| 86 EVEN | 87 BREGUET | BISSEY | PEUTAT | 04-05/08/1944 | N Bièvre, 6 km S Orbais l'Abbaye (Marne) |
| 89 VERMUGE | 88 ROGIER | MOCQUET | L BIGNON | | |
| 90 LAVILLE | 91 BUGEAUD | ROSSEXELLE | RIGNON | | |
| 92 MORVAL | 93 MARCHAND | MORILLON | LAFONTAINE | | |
| 94 COULOMBEL | 95 FOUQUET | BACQUET | DARQUES | 04-05/08/1944 | 2 km N Lorrez-le-Bocage DZ La Croix Blanche (Seine et Mar… |
| 96 COULON | 97 PUISSEGUR | CAMBON | MOREAU | 08/09/1944 | S E Bouzanville - 10 km N Mirecourt DZ Restaurant (Vosges) |
| 51 KERGOUR | 52 DUJARDIN | DE BEAUCORPS | BARRE | 01-02/09/1944 | S E Bouzanville - 10 km N Mirecourt DZ Restaurant (Vosges) |
| 57 BLANC | 58 VERNEZ | DE SORBIER | RAVARRE | | |
| 98 BERTHET | 99 REGNIER | BARTHELEMY | FAIVRE | 01-02/09/1944 | Entre Haillanville & Fauconcourt, 10 km Nord-Ouest Ramberv… DZ Saltimbanque (Vosges) |
| 45 LAURENT | 32 BOISSIER | RIGOT | PEDRO | 03-04/09/1944 | 5 Km N E Nogent en Bassigny (Haute Marne) |

| | |
|---|---|
| † | Killed Action |
| P | Prisoner of war liberated at the end of the war |
| PNR | Prisoner of war, missing |

| LIEU | CODE MISSION | OSSEX | BRISSEX | EQUIPAGE | OPERATION | RAF | USAAF |
|---|---|---|---|---|---|---|---|
| PARIS | PATHFINDERS | | BRISSEX | RAF Sqn 161 - F/L Parker | Calanque | 2 | |
| | | | BRISSEX | | | 2 | |
| ROUEN | BERTHIER | | BRISSEX | | | 2 | |
| AMIENS | DROLOT | | BRISSEX | RAF Sqn 161 - F/L Caldwell | Tempete (Banane) | 2 | |
| LE MANS | PLAINCHANT | OSSEX | | | | 2 | |
| CHARTRES | VITRAIL | OSSEX | | | | 2 | |
| ORLEANS | JEANNE | OSSEX | | RAF Sqn 138 - F/Sgt Jones | Ouragan (Citron & Mirabelle) | 2 | |
| PARIS OUEST | LEFEVRE | | BRISSEX | | | 2 | |
| MELUN | PLUTARQUE | OSSEX | | Carpetbaggers St Clair MR393 | Plymouth 2 | | 2 |
| ROMILLY / AUBE | EVASION | OSSEX | | Carpetbaggers Fish MR394 | Ellis 3 | | 2 |
| PARIS | PATHFINDERS II | | BRISSEX | RAF | | 2 | |
| EVREUX | NEY | | BRISSEX | Carpetbaggers Stapel MR429 A | Fiat 6 | | 2 |
| ETAMPES | DIANE | OSSEX | | | | | 2 |
| LE BOURGET | CHARLES | OSSEX | | | | | 2 |
| NORD | JUNOT | | BRISSEX | Carpetbaggers Kelly MR485 | Austin 3 | | 2 |
| LILLE | FOY | | BRISSEX | | | | 2 |
| BLOIS | VIS | OSSEX | | | | | 2 |
| VERSAILLES | MARBOT | | BRISSEX | Carpetbaggers RABBITT MR550 | Cord 1 | | 2 |
| TOURS | CURE | OSSEX | | | | | 2 |
| VINCENNES | MADELEINE | OSSEX | | Carpetbaggers MERRILL MR0536 | | | 2 |
| SAUMUR | JUSTICE | OSSEX | | RAF Sqn 161 Caldwell | Charite | 2 | |
| VAIRES / MARNE | CENDRILLON | OSSEX | | Carpetbaggers PIKE MR617 | Donald 8B | | 2 |
| JUVISY | FOUDRE | OSSEX | | Carpetbaggers Mc Kee MR618 | Donald 5 | | 2 |
| St POL DE LEON | CERCLE | OSSEX | | RAF Sqn 161 - Cpt Piltingsrud | Harry 21 (Ex Lincoln ) | 2 | |
| RENNES | PAPIER | OSSEX | | Carpetbaggers MERRILL MR821 | | | 2 |
| VENDOME | COLERE | OSSEX | | | | | 1 |
| LAVAL | SALAUD | OSSEX | | Carpetbaggers HEFLIN MR826 | Ansaldo 1 | | 2 |
| VENDOME | FILAN | OSSEX | | | | | 2 |
| VENDOME | COLERE | OSSEX | | RAF | | | 1 |
| SOISSONS | MURAT | | BRISSEX | RAF 161 (F/lt Caldwell) | Donald 6 | 2 | |
| BEAUVAIS | LANNES | | BRISSEX | | | 2 | |
| EPERNAY | COUPE | OSSEX | | | | 2 | |
| NORD CASSEL | SOULT | | BRISSEX | RAF Sqn 161 - F/Lt Loos | Palaiseau | 2 | |
| TROYES | HELENE | OSSEX | | | | 2 | |
| VALENCIENNES | GROUCHY | | BRISSEX | | | 2 | |
| ALENCON | DENTELLE | OSSEX | | RAF (ex Desoto 1 - Carpetbaggers) | | 2 | |
| BOURGES | SANCTUAIRE | OSSEX | | RAF | | 2 | |
| MANTES | KELLERMAN | | BRISSEX | | | 2 | |
| ST QUENTIN | DAVOUST | | BRISSEX | RAF Sqn 138 - F/L Kidd | Parapluie | 2 | |
| AIRES/LA LYS | MARMONT | | BRISSEX | | | 2 | |
| ST GERMAIN | BEAUHARNAIS | | BRISSEX | | | 2 | |
| MAUBEUGE | DESAIX | | BRISSEX | | | 2 | |
| CAMBRAI | OUDINOT | | BRISSEX | RAF Sqn 138 - F/L Palmer | Martini | 2 | |
| ARRAS | JOURDAN | | BRISSEX | | | 2 | |
| ROUBAIX | RAPP | | BRISSEX | | | 2 | |
| REIMS | KLEBER | | BRISSEX | | | 2 | |
| SEZANNE | DARU | | BRISSEX | RAF Sqn 161 F/Lt Johnston | Mexico | 2 | |
| LAON | BERTHOLLET | | BRISSEX | | | 2 | |
| DIJON | EPICE | OSSEX | | | | 2 | |
| MONTARGIS | LAPIN | OSSEX | | Carpetbaggers Sanders MR1430 | Benz 1 | | 2 |
| NEUFCHATEAU | DIAMANT | OSSEX | | Carpetbaggers Byerley MR1801 | Bob 277 | | 2 |
| BESANCON | OR | OSSEX (1) | | Carpetbaggers Coleman MR1837 – Bob 277 | Bob 277 | | 2 |
| MONTBELLIARD | MONTRE | OSSEX (1) | | | | | 2 |
| RAMBERVILLIERS | VELOURS | OSSEX | | Carpetbaggers Bales MR1847 | Bob 279 | | 2 |
| LANGRES | OUTIL | OSSEX (1) | | Carpetbaggers Gwiazdon MR1911 | Bob 335 | | 2 |
| (1) 2nd drop | | 29 | 25 | | | 62 | 46 |
| | | 54 | | | | 108 | |

# THE "PATHFINDER" MISSION

1944

*Above.*
**Lieutenant Jeannette Guyot GM a.k.a "Jeannette", was the first Sussex agent of the first "Pathfinder" mission. She jumped during the night of 8 to 9 February 1944 on the Loches DZ in the Indre et Loire département alongside three other agents.**
*(Sussex picture collection)*

*Top right.*
**Lieutenant Georges Lassalle a.k.a "Lescour", radio operator of the "Pathfinder" mission.**
*(Sussex picture collection)*

On 8 February 1944, the first two missions, named "Pathfinder" were parachuted over Loches in the Indre-et-Loire département. Those teams were made up of four officers: Jeannette Guyot, Marcel Saubestre, Georges Lasalle and Pierre Binet.

Their mission was to locate future landing and dropping zones, to establish contact with sympathisers, to prepare caches for the equipment and so on. In the next six months and thanks to a lot of hard work, they located and organised 22 dropping zones, including 17 that were to be used operationally, some of them twice. They also listed close to one hundred "safe houses" were Sussex agents would be able to seek refuge.

Arriving in Paris with Georges Lasalle, the team's radio operator Jeannette decided to visit her cousin, madame Kiehl at the "Café de l'Electricité" in Faubourg Montmartre. They were made most welcome. After a few days, Jeannette was housed by Andrée Goubillon, a friend, whose husband was held as a POW. She owned a café located at 8, rue Tournefort in Paris. When liberation came, this café was renamed "Café Sussex". This is what madame Goubillon had to say about Jeannette when she was interviewed just before she passed away in October 1988:

*"I knew what she was up to and when she asked me whether I was ready to help, I did not think twice about it and said yes. Even though the café was located close to a Gestapo office, I knew what I had to do and I was not afraid."*

This is how the dangerous and difficult job of giving shelter to some Sussex teams began. Madame Goubillon remembered that when an agent first initiated contact with her in her café, he would start by asking *"Hello auntie, how is my uncle doing?"* At the same time, they would show the picture of a baby who was known under the name of Mic-Mic and who in fact was the last born of "colonel Rémy". The two "Pathfinder" teams had a number of hairy moments; their mission was fraught with unpredic-

table incidents but they still managed to carry it out successfully. In that permanent David vs. Goliath struggle, danger was a constant companion and one had to learn how to live with it.

Georges Lasalle, the radio operator, was once located by the German direction finding unit after having emitted for too long a period from the same position.

The Germans kicked his door in and Lasalle was immediately immobilized to make sure he would not swallow his cyanide pill. At once, one of the policemen asked him *"Where is the radio operator?"* Lasalle immediately answered, *"He has just jumped out the window"*. Seeing that the window really was open, the Germans ran after this "ghost" radio operator while in fact they were already detaining him. Nevertheless, this did not save him from extensive torture cessions. In order to buy time and not be executed immediately, Lassale started inventing imaginary agents and networks to such an extent that on a given day, the Gestapo agents took him

to the city of La Rochelle where, according to his stories, he had once established contact with several résistance fighters. Lassale was then kept at the Gestapo's disposal and imprisoned in the Fresnes prison in Paris.

At the beginning of August, he established contact with several French prison wardens. He told them that the Free French in London knew their identities and that he could, if they helped him escape, vouch for them when France was to be eventually liberated. If they refused to assist him and the other inmates that were kept with him on death row to escape, he guaranteed the wardens that they would be tracked and slaughtered with their families by the liberators.

This is how Georges Lassalle lived to see the liberation of Paris. Pierre Binet was not that lucky. Arrested by the Germans, he was executed in the Othe forest, not far from the city of Troyes, on 28 August 1944 with another French patriot named Ancergues.

*Above.*
*Lieutenant Lucien Binet a.k.a "Lucien". On 28 August 1944, he was shot by the Germans with Ancergue a.k.a "Asnier" who belonged to the "Pathfinder 2" mission.*
*(Sussex picture collection)*

*Top left.*
*Commandant (Major) Marcel Saubestre a.k.a "Marcel", mission commander for "Pathfinder". Often operating from madame Andrée's café, "Marcel" provided constant support to Sussex teams transiting through Paris. The cellar of what would later be known as café Sussex was used to store equipment, weapons and radio sets.*
*(Sussex picture collection)*

*Opposite.*
**A post war picture of Georges Lassalle as a Colonial infantry Captain sporting his Sussex badge as well as his French and allied decorations. First row (French decorations): chevalier de la Légion d'Honneur, médaille militaire, croix de guerre 1939-1945 avec palme, médaille de la résistance ; second row ( allied awards) Distinguished Service Order (UK) Distinguished Service Cross (USA).**
*(Sussex picture collection)*

*Below.*
**Commandant Marcel Saubestre's end-of-mission report typed on 4 September 1944.**
*(Sussex picture collection)*

*Opposite.*
**Jeannette on the ground in her SOE jumpsuit and Sorbo helmet and a fully inflated American-made parachute.**
*(Jeannette Guyot picture – Sussex collection)*

*Opposite.*
**Jeannette Guyot's La George Medal.**
*(Sussex picture collection)*

*Above.*
**Jeannette Guyot's enlistment certificate in the Free French Forces.**
*(Sussex picture collection)*

*Below and Opposite.*
**Jeannette Guyot wearing the Sussex insignia as a brooch. Jeannette Guyot was one of only two women awarded the American Distinguished Service Cross in World War II or since. Virginia Hall, the other woman, was a U.S. Civilian working for the O.S.S.**
*(Jeannette Guyot/Sussex picture collection)*

FORCES FRANÇAISES LIBRES

### ACTE D'ENGAGEMENT

No. de l'engagement 0649

Par devant nous, (1) Colonel BILLOTTE
représentant le Général de Gaulle, Commandant en Chef les Forces Françaises Libres,
a comparu M. (2) Melle JANIN alias GAUTHIER Jeannette

M. (2) Melle JANIN alias GAUTHIER Jeannette, déclaré :
—avoir pris connaissance du statut du personnel des Forces Françaises Libres ;
—s'engager à servir avec Honneur, Fidélité et Discipline dans les Forces Françaises Libres pour la durée de la guerre actuellement en cours plus trois mois.

Le présent engagement est définitif sous réserve :
1° du résultat favorable de l'examen médical ;
2° de l'accord de l'État Major Particulier du Général de Gaulle ;
lesquels devront être obtenus dans un délai maximum de 42 jours.

à Londres le 14 Mai 1945

Lu et approuvé (3)
Le (4) Le Colonel

L'engagé
Signature de deux témoins

Le présent contrat
la date du
L'INTENDANT MILITAIRE

(1) nom de l'Intendant Militaire ou de l'Officier en faisant fonction.
(2) nom et prénom de l'engagé.
(3) mention à porter en toutes lettres de la main de l'engagé.
(4) Grade et nom de l'Intendant ou de l'Officier en faisant fonction.
L'acte d'engagement est établi en deux exemplaires :
L'exemplaire blanc est à conserver par le Bureau des Effectifs.
L'exemplaire bleu est à remettre à l'engagé.

41

Capitaine William Bechtel MC a.k.a "Louis Bonnet" who belonged to the "Berthier" mission. On 1 July 1940, in London, he joined the Free French forces (recruiting number 361 A). Confirmed in his rank of Lieutenant on 25 September 1940, Bechtel was posted to the 2e Bataillon de Marches de l'Oubangui-Chari in Bangui in French Equatorial Africa (AEF, now the Central African Republic). He took part in the Syria campaign as well as in some policing operations in the Euphrates region and in the Libya campaign. He fought in Bir-Hakeim, was promoted to the rank of Captain on 25 March 1943 and volunteered for a transfer to the BCRA. He arrived in London in September 1943. On 1 October, he was posted to the Sussex plan and sent to St Alban.
*(Sussex picture collection)*

*Opposite.*
**Commandant William Bechtel's garrison corp.**
*(Sussex picture collection)*

# THE "BERTHIER" MISSION

BRISSEX
BCRA

## Parachuted on 9 April 1944 over Neuvy-Pailloux (Indre département)
Area of operation: Rouen
End of mission: on liberation of the city of Rouen
Captain William Bechtel a.k.a "Louis Bonnet"
Lieutenant Viarnaud a.k.a "Vallade"

EXTRACT from the memories of William Bechtel :
During his mission, while riding a bicycle, "Louis Bonnet" came across a very large German convoy which was driving at considerable speed towards the city. Without thinking twice about it, "Bonnet" managed to approach a German truck and to finally hold on to it; to all, he appeared like he was freeloading in order to help him go across a steep hill. Inside the truck were probably about twenty German soldiers, seating face to face; many looked asleep, resting on their Mauser rifles, their heads rolling with the movements of the truck. Seeing how "Bonnet" was hitching a ride, the two NCOs who were seating at the back shouted immediately:

- Los ! Los !

Keeping his head cool, "Bonnet" relied on his linguistic skills:

- Ich bin ein Elsässer ! [1]

-Ach so ! answered the NCOs who had initially displayed the most aggression.

For several minutes, "Bonnet" and the two NCOs had the most unlikely conversation. For the Germans, "Bonnet" must have appeared as a completely harmless lunatic who just used the German convoy to move faster. True, he did not want to be late for the contact with Marius and since the S-Phone was hidden in the château, this most unexpected German assistance was more than welcome.

Unfortunately, soon before the Malaunay viaduct, "Bonnet" fell into a shell hole he had not spotted in the darkness. He immediately felt a shooting pain in the top part of his left leg; he did all he could not to scream in pain. The truck which he had held on to had stopped immediately; in a second, "Bonnet" understood the seriousness of his situation. If the Germans were to take too keen an interest on his injury, he was finished. In his pockets, "Bonnet" had several maps of the area, coded messages, his own "flash code" as well as some batteries for his radio set lashed to his bicycle. Mustering all his energy, "Bonnet" managed to stand up; using his bicycle as support, he managed to keep on walking for about twenty metres, waving to the Germans; when he came closer to them, he managed to shout:

- *Es geht, kein problem.* [2]
- *Are you in much pain?*

Hiding in the shadows, a man had called to "Louis Bonnet" who was by then laying flat on the ground. Without even waiting for the answer, the man started helping him back on his feet.

Who was he? Friend of foe?

Would "Bonnet's" career as a secret agent end because of a stupid shell hole? He had always been so lucky until then…

- *First the bike, hide the bike!* said "Bonnet" who was still in a lot of pain.

The man hesitated for an instant; he then took the bicycle and pushed it for a short distance, to a nearby café. He then came back to fetch "Bonnet". The German convoy was still passing on the road.

"Bonnet" had just been taken to the café and the man who had cared for him appeared to be on his own.

- *My name is Martin and you should not even bother trying to tell me you were just on a leisurely ride….*

"Bonnet" understood he was dealing with a patriot, a man who could be trusted; anyway, he had little choice.

- *I have got some mates with the Résistance,* we'll sort that out said Martin in a hushed voice.

"Bonnet" had to destroy all the incriminating documents he held. He insisted that Martin destroyed the maps, the messages and the "flash-code". With great care, the café owner burnt in his chimney all the bits and pieces that could have proved difficult to explain. Lying on a bench in the garden, "Bonnet" was in constant pain in spite of the strong liquor Martin had given him.

The café owner was now on the phone, calling a certain monsieur Baron. Through the open door, "Bonnet" understood their were talking about ambulance and hospital.

- *"They" will be there in an hour!* said Martin with a smile.

The agent motioned Martin forward.

- *I owe you a lot you know…* you won't regret this!

While saying this "Bonnet" had put his hand inside his pocket and had produced several banknotes. Martin leaned on "Bonnet's" shoulder and told him with a smile:

- *No, I am really doing this for France…*

"Bonnet" understood there was not point in insisting. Martin would not accept any compensation for the risks he had taken.

*Opposite.*
**Lieutenant Viarnaud a.k.a "Vallado", radio de William Bechtel's radio operator.**
*(Sussex picture collection)*

1- I am an Alsatian.
2- It's all good, no problem.

43

waiting for him. He offered for "Louis Bonnet" to be taken to the private hospital of his friend doctor Dessaint.

The surgeon quickly examined "Bonnet" and diagnosed him with a broken femoral neck. The doctor soon understood "Bonnet" was no ordinary patient; he was thus accommodated in a single room, away from the daily hustle-bustle of the hospital staff. The severity of his injury demanded an operation, which had to be conducted in the best possible time. This did not please "Bonnet" much as he did not wanted to have to interrupt his mission. On his second day in the clinic, he asked to see the surgeon privately.

- *Doctor, please give me a straight answer to the question I a going to ask you, even if you may find it strange.*
- *Of course monsieur Bonnet*, answered the doctor.
- *What if you cut off my leg? I heard that the healing process would be quicker!*
- *You must be joking monsieur Bonnet…*
- *No, I am not answered* "Bonnet".
- *Then you must be stark raving mad.*

The doctor left "Bonnet"'s bedroom thinking his friend Hatt knew some rather curious people. "Bonnet" had his operation on 7 August. The cast doctor Dessaint had used was impressive and it immobilised his leg from the waist down. As soon as he woke up, "Louis Bonnet" asked the nurse if she could tell Mr. Hatt he needed to speak with him. Less than an hour later, he was standing in front of him.

- *How are you feeling? You gave us all hell of a fright* he said as an introduction.
- *Have you told my other contacts about my situation?* was "Bonne"'s only answer.
- *I had thought that considering the sorry state you are in…*
- *But my dear Hatt, the war goes on* answered "Bonnet".

Mr. Hatt soon understood that the indomitable "Bonnet" was not going to let this situation phase him. Without wasting any additional time, he told the young Alsatian girl and the castle owner that he had feared the worst had happened when he had not returned. As early as the 8th of August, "Bonnet" had reorganised his network in relation to the condition and position he now was finding himself in. Everyday, those two key agents were visiting him at the hospital in order to transmit the information they had gathered. Bed bound, "Bonnet" spent hours coding messages; he then handed them over

- *Do you have a bike? asked* "Bonnet".
- *No*, answered Martin who understood what was coming.

It was thus decided that "Louis Bonnet" would leave his bicycle for Martin to use as a token of his gratitude. A few minutes later, "Bonnet" left Malaunay in a "défense passive" (civilian protection service) ambulance. Martin's friend, monsieur Baron, was driving the vehicle. In Rouen, monsieur Hatt, who had been warned through the telephone, was

PRÉSIDENCE
DU GOUVERNEMENT PROVISOIRE
Services de la Défense Nationale

RÉPUBLIQUE FRANÇAISE
LIBERTÉ - ÉGALITÉ - FRATERNITÉ

DIRECTION GÉNÉRALE
DES ÉTUDES & RECHERCHES
(D.G.E.R.)

Paris, le 9 Janvier 1945

ORDRE DE MISSION Nº 2803

IL EST PRESCRIT A :

NOM  BECHTEL

PRÉNOM  William

NÉ LE  1er octobre 1904  EPINAL  (Vosges)

NATIONALITÉ  Française

GRADE & FONCTIONS  Capitaine

DÉTENTEUR DE LA CARTE D'IDENTITÉ Nº  DÉLIVRÉE PAR

A PRÉSENTER AVEC LE PRÉSENT ORDRE

DOMICILIÉ A  PARIS  (34 Rue de L'Université)

DE SE RENDRE A :  ROUEN

ITINÉRAIRE

MOYENS de TRANSPORT  VOITURE  467 F.F.E.E.  ou 8260 BАВ  conduite par

DATE de DÉPART  le Lieutenant Joyeuse.

DATE de RETOUR  Mission terminée.

Les autorités françaises et alliées, civiles et militaires sont priées de faciliter à l'intéressé l'accomplissement de sa mission.

LE Lt-Colonel MANUEL,
Directeur Technique
SIGNATURE(1)  (fonctions)

T.S.V.P.

IDENTITY CARD

FOREIGN OFFICER

Serial Nº 09927

AVAILABLE IN GREAT BRITAIN
AND NORTHERN IRELAND

Photograph of Holder.

Signature of Holder

*Above.*
**Parachute log book belonging to William Bechtel; the picture on the right shows, written in red ink, the entry for the operational jump he did over Châteauroux during the night of the 4th of April 1944 at the beginning of the "Berthier" mission.**
(Sussex picture collection)

to "Vallade" who transmitted them to London. This peculiar organisation lasted for nine days without any glitch. On the ninth day, while Dr Dessaint did his daily visit to the patients, "Bonnet" told him he would leave the hospital on this very evening.

- But you are completely unfit to travel monsieur Bonnet, I am positive …

The doctor kept on repeating, "unfit to travel", nodding his head while "Bonnet" was already explaining the details of the evening's operation.

- I will take a vehicle belonging to the "défense passive" said "Bonnet" with a big grin and a quiet demeanour.

"Louis Bonnet" had estimated that he just could not stay idle in this hospital anymore. Moreover, he did not want to be a source of problems for doctor Dessaint who had taken such good care of him.

*Above.*
*William Bechtel's post-WW2 French parachute wings # 4631and medal ribbons including the following awards: Légion d'Honneur, médaille Militaire, médaille de la Résistance (Officier), Croix de guerre de 1914-1918 with 2 citations, Croix de guerre 1939-1945 with 2 citations, médaille de la France Libre, médaille coloniale with "Bir-Hakeim" and "Extrême-Orient" clasps, médaille commémorative 39-45, médaille des engagés volontaires en 1914, médaille des Blessés, Military Cross (UK) and médaille de l'Ordre du Liban (Lebanon).*
*(Sussex picture collection)*

Soon before the curfew, the "défense passive" lorry pulled in front of the visitor's entrance of the hospital. The duty nurse took some convincing before she let "Bonnet" board the ancient vehicle. She demanded the approval of doctor Dessaint before waving him off. The "défense passive" female assistant had three young volunteer stretcher bearers with her, complete with duty armband. When the duty nurse had finally spoken to Dessaint on the phone and that he had given his approval, she reluctantly told the "défense passive" team:

- Monsieur Bonnet is now better…so I have been told….

The nurse understood there was not point in insisting and she let the team load the patient in the lorry.

Doctor Dessaint had never been under any illusion about the real nature of "Bonnet's" activities and he had done what he could to help him in the daily activities that had nothing to do with his medical recovery.

During the period he spent in hospital, "Louis Bonnet" had never told London about his predicament. Except on the day he was operated on, his messages had been sent as scheduled.

The young teacher who had been asked if he could house "Bonnet" accepted immediately. She offered her own bedroom so he could be made more at ease but before that, climbing the five floors to her flat was a bit of an epic. Mademoiselle Opérie and her colleague mademoiselle Koenig did all they could to insure "Louis Bonnet" was comfortable. With his bed emplaced directly in front of a window, he had a grandstand view of the city of Rouen.

From 16 August 1944 to the liberation of Rouen on 1 September 1944, Louis Bonnet was to live with those two young women. Once "Bonnet" had shown her how to proceed, the young Alsatian girl proved to be of great help to code the messages, worked both confidently and quickly.

On the Normandy Front, the Germans were now in full retreat towards the river Seine. The armoured vehicles, artillery pieces and lorries that had managed to escape the Caen plains were now the targets of the Allied air forces. From May 1944, 800 air attacks had destroyed the bridges over the river Seine.

On 25 August, the US 15th Corps reached Elbeuf, a few kilometres South of Rouen. The day before, the Canadians had occupied Lisieux and they were now pushing towards the Basse-Normandie département. In conjunction with the British 2nd Army, they were encircling the Brotonne forest in which the remains of six Germans divisions belonging to the VIIe Army were hiding.

On 29 August, the Canadians were in sight of Rouen. The German rear guards were fighting ferociously to prevent the remains of von Kluge's army from encirclement. In just a few days, the surviving

*Opposite.*
**MK XXI emergency transceiver used during the**
**"Dentelles" mission in the city of Alençon by Lieutenant**
**Pierre Ravarre a.k.a "Vernez" in July 1944.**
*(Georges Ducreuzet picture)*

VII Army's heavy assets had all converged to the loop of the river Seine located South of Rouen. In this cul-de-sac, and particularly on the Cavelier de La Salle and Jean de Béthencourt quays, a monstrous traffic jam had developed. Hours after hours, thousands of vehicles of all descriptions kept on arriving, packing the roads and streets of the left bank of the Seine. The night before, "Bonnet" had sent a situation report as well as the grid coordinates of the main German troop concentrations. Feeling that the end was near, the network was working full steam and "Bonnet's" bed was littered with messages. He had never received such an incredible amount of intelligence in such a short period.

The next day, soon before midday, the wail of sirens was heard. The air raid warning was lifted an hour later without any sign of Allied air activity in the sky over Rouen. Seeing the tanks and vehicles

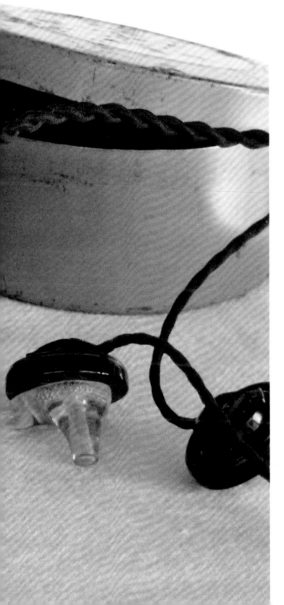

massed in front of the destroyed bridges, "Bonnet" could feel that the different pieces of the tragedy were slowly getting into places. Lying in his bed in front of the window, "Bonnet" was waiting. He somehow knew that the grand final would be on par with the rest of events: simply phenomenal!

At 1930 hours, the Rouen sirens wailed for the last time of the war. A few minutes later, at precisely 1935 hours, the cataclysm started. RAF bombers dove on the German troop and vehicle concentrations, dropping 150 bombs along the quaysides. In a few minutes, the pride of the German war machine, which had sown death all around Europe, was turned into burning hulks of metal. All that was left were mangled and twisted pieces of metal in a sea of flames.....

Destruction was everywhere. General von Kluge's VIIth Army had ceased to exist in an infernal apotheosis. From his window, "Louis Bonnet" had witnessed the destruction. Mademoiselle Opérie's house shook under the blast of the bombs and secondary explosions. Bed-bound, "Bonnet" thought at one point that the house was just about to collapse and that he was going to disappear in the fire and steel inferno he had contributed to unleash.

When the first waves of bombers appeared, "Bonnet" called mademoiselle Opérie who was busy in her kitchen.

- Come! shouted "Bonnet" who could see the first planes just about to dive on their targets.

- Sorry monsieur Bonnet, I just can't, or else my tomatoes will burn!

Mademoiselle Opérie remained true to herself, not the one to be easily phased. In the evening, as a conclusion, "Louis Bonnet" sent the following message to Marius:

- Apart from my radio operator and I, there are no more military objectives in Rouen!

The "Berthier" mission was over.

*Opposite.*
**Multi-bladed escape knife with pliers which belonged to Pierre Vergès d'Espagne a.k.a "capitaine Le Teyrac".**
**Markings: RD N° 354051.**
*(Sussex picture collection)*

*Opposite.*
**"Pattern 39" Battle Dress worn in St Albans by Sussex trainees. The agents were all recruited as P2 agents with the rank of Second Lieutenant except for a few older career officers who kept their ranks. On this picture, the "France" title is printed in white over khaki material.**
*(Sussex picture collection)*

*Below.*
**Sussex teams were issued large sums of money in banknotes in order to be able to pay informants or, when needed, buy equipment (bicycle or car tires, wood-fired engines...)**
*(Sussex picture collection)*

# 1944 THE "PLAINCHANT" MISSION

OSSEX
BCRA

Parachuted on 9 April 1944 in Neuvy-Pailloux (Indre département)
Area of operation: Le Mans
Lieutenant Georges Clément a.k.a "Georges Clauzel"
Lieutenant Henri Vergon a.k.a "André Coulon"
End of mission: on liberation of the city of Le Mans on 8 August 1944
Henri Vergon was recovered on 10 August 1944 by Justin O'Brien.

THIS TEAM, which was parachuted during the night of 9 to 10 April 1944 sent a sizeable number of messages on different objectives such as V1 launching sites or the location of the HQs of the "Das Reich" and "Hohenstaufen" SS-Panzer Divisions; they also reported the suicide of General F. Dollman who was in command of the Le Mans area for the VIIth Army.

Like many other Sussex teams, the "Plainchant" mission had been issued with an S-Phone. Georges, who used this device regularly, only learnt later that the man who answered his radio messages was the famous French writer and journalist Joseph Kessel who was then part of the Sussex squadron (the RAF's 226 Squadron). Interviewed on 6 June 1984 by Patricia Cleveland Peck, a BBC journalist, for a broadcast on the occasion of the 40th anniversary of Operation Overlord, Georges then told this interesting anecdote:

*A few days before he was arrested, while liaising with madame Andrée Goubillon, the owner of a café located rue Tournefort in Paris, Georges had bet with her that Paris would be liberated on 15 August and that they would have dinner together on that day to celebrate the event!*

Unluckily for him, Georges was arrested by the Germans rue Charcot in Le Mans on the evening of the 27th of July. In his bedroom, the Gestapo found a radio set as well as a large sum of money (40,000 francs). Sent by the Germans to the Fresnes prison, he was interrogated until the 10th of August. In spite of ill treatments and torture, he refused to speak. On 15th August, his captors decided to deport him to Germany. A bus convoy ferried the prisoners from the Fresnes prison to the Pantin train station in Paris. Once in the station, Georges Clément scribbled a note on a piece of paper and threw it on the railway. A railroad employee picked it up discreetly; the note was addressed to madame Goubillon, 8 rue Tournefort, Paris Ve, and it read:

*"Been arrested – Sent to Germany – sorry about today's meal – Best wishes - Georges from Le Mans."*

*Opposite.*
**Lieutenant Henri Vergon a.k.a "Coulon", the Plainchant mission radio operator.**
*(Sussex picture collection)*

A note in the OSS archives conclude that on the date the report was drafted, there was no way to know if Georges Clément was dead or alive…

In fact, Georges Clément came back alive from captivity and received the american *Distinguished Service Cross* for his service.

*Opposite.*
**Lieutenant Georges Clément a.k.a Georges Clauzel,**
**the Plainchant mission radio operator.**
*(Sussex picture collection)*

*Opposite.*
**The hastily scribbled note Georges Clément a.k.a**
**"Georges Clauzel" managed to throw out of the**
**train which took him from the gare de Pantin**
**station in Paris to a concentration camp in**
**Germany after he was arrested by the Gestapo.**
**This note was found by an unknown person who**
**brought it to the café of madame André Goubillon**
**in Paris. It reads as such: "Been arrested - Leaving**
**for Germany — So much for today's lunch — Best**
**wishes - Georges from Le Mans."**
*(Sussex Collection)*

*Opposite.*
**226 Squadron RAF badge. This squadron was sometimes called the «Sussex Squadron».**

*Opposite.*
**The famous journalist and writer Joseph Kessel.
And his friend André Bernheim were incorporated to 226 Squadron. Flying on B-25 Mitchell bombers, they established voice communication through S-Phones with Sussex teams on the ground. Those teams could relay near real-time intelligence on the enemy, bringing close air support and artillery fire on German armour and troops movement on several occasions.**
*(Sussex picture collection)*

*Below.*
**Madame Andrée Goubillon's café. She was affectionately known as "la Maman" by those who were by then called "Les Sussex". Located rue Tournefort in the 5th arrondissement of Paris, this café was used as a rendezvous point and weapons, radio and equipment cache by Sussex teams transiting through Paris. After the war, as a sign of their affection and gratefulness, British MI6 agents offered to repaint and rename the café as the "Café" du Réseau Sussex" (Sussex network café). After the war, and until "la Maman" passed away, on the first Friday of every month, a table was reserved for the members of the Amicale du Plan Sussex, the Sussex plan Old Comrades association.**
*(Sussex picture collection)*

# THE "CHARLES" MISSION

OSSEX
BCRA

**Parachuted on 28 May 1944 over Nicorbin (4 km North of Voves), Eure & Loire département.**

Area of operation : Le Bourget (a Paris suburb famous for its airport).
End of mission 1st of September 1944
Observer: Lieutenant René Veuve a.k.a Joyeuse
Radio operator : Georges Ducasse a.k.a Chaloner

*Opposite.*
**Lieutenant Georges Ducasse, a.k.a "Chaloner".**
*(Sussex picture collection)*

THIS TEAM WAS TO PROVIDE a host of information on the Le Bourget airport, the Dugny-La-Courneuve aviation-grade oil refinery as well as on regional railway traffic, cargo traffic on the Seine river, underground networks and quarries in the North of Paris as well as on the development of new weapons at the navy powder establishment located in the city of Sevran.

Since the team had just fired two of its informants as it had doubts about their reliability, it started looking into the development of another network of human sources when "Joyeuse" was introduced to Fritz Laemmerschmidt, a former Luftwaffe technical inspector who had by then been AWOL for over a year. He was completely opposed to the National –Socialist ideology and he soon became a precious informant, providing a number of very important intelligence reports. The team also helped him in producing posters inciting Wehrmacht soldiers to desert. 80,000 francs were taken from the Sussex funds for this particular operation and this money was instrumental in the production of fifty thousand of those posters that were placed on the walls of the French capital, with immediate results on the morale of the occupying forces.

The end of mission report of the Charles mission also mentions the following :

"I was also introduced by capitaine Bechtel to a man who was known as "Athos". He had met him in the city of Rouen, an area he had had to leave in a hurry since he was being hunted by the Gestapo. He was after different set of technical informations and blueprints, all vital for the Allies, including the V1 and V2 and the manned torpedo. He was supposed to have organized a deal to buy those plans from a German feldwebel but things turned out differently.

Pushing the feldwebel and one of his comrades hard to get those documents, he finally ended up breaking into the Gestapo safe himself. Believing he was stealing secret documents, he in fact stole no less than 13 million francs ! Acting in good faith, he immediately gave the Service one million francs that I distributed to several teams including Marcel, commandant Ledron, Charrot and the local Forces Françaises de l'Intérieur. But the heist had been reported and while trying to change some of that money, "Athos" was arrested buy the French Sureté Française and sent to the judiciary police prison where he still is today."

Unfortunately, some more serious incidents were to make René Veuve's and Georges Ducasse's tasks more complicated.

On Sunday 13 August, the local Front National having organized a little get together in honour of the advancing Allied forces, the Forces Françaises de l'Intérieur, believing their moment of glory had arrived, launched a premature operation with two civilian cars packed with armed FFI members. The Germans got wind of that movement and met the FFI head on; a shoot-out followed and the under-gunned FFI withdrew which left the German forces plenty of time to start a wide search operation of the district where both the S-Phone and the headquarters of Veuve were located. In order to escape the German forces, Veuve had to spent most of his Sunday in the underground sewer system; he soon realized it was safer to leave the area of Livry-Gargan with his radio set altogether since he also had been "DF'ed" by the Gestapo direction-finding unit.

René Veuve takes up the story: This explains why I had to undertake that somewhat hazardous movement of my radio equipment to the city of Aulnay-Sous-Bois, at the home of Doctor Perlis located 5 rue Dumont. This was an ideal location for radio emissions and I operated from there for several days, until the night of the 17th to the 18th of August.

On that evening, returning to the Doctor's house around 2230 hours, I linked up with the two FFI who acted as my protection detail whenever I broadcasted,

Louis Barault and Pierre Gastaud. Dr Perlis'maid was in her bedroom on the first floor.

I set up my radio equipment and around quarter to one, the two FFIs took up their watch positions outside the house as they usually did. The quality of the radio contact was very poor; I spent the longest time fine tuning my set and finally the contact was over around quarter past two. For over thirty minutes, I was not feeling quite right, feeling like there was an hostile presence outside the house. I tried to reason myself and then walked out and asked the two FFIs whether they had seen or heard anything untowards. They answered everything was fine and normal. Nevertheless, my uneasy feeling kept on growing and I peered into the darkness in order to confirm all was well. Doing this, I thought I saw a shadow where the wall linked with Dr. Perlis' home. I quietly pointed it out to the FFIs who told me it was nothing but the rush of the wind in the leaves.

As I peered from the balcony, I suddenly was caught in the beam of a powerful torch. I was then in shirtsleeves and socks; I immediately realized the house had been surrounded and told the FFIs " we are surrounded, let's get quickly out of here". As I walked back into the house where I had set up my radio equipment to grab my .45 Colt pistol, four German stick grenades were thrown into the room through the still open window. It was too late to recover my "Klaxon" (this is how I called my radio set). I latter learned it was damaged by the grenade explosions that also threw me off my feet twice even though they left me unscathed save for a nick on my right big toe.

We all ran for the corridor in order to reach the little staircase located in the back of the house. We managed to leave the house just as the Boches were entering through the garden gate. They seemed to be everywhere, in the "Secours National" park and in the streets around Dr. Perlis' house. We jumped over the first fence of the park together and ran across the lawns hoping to reach the railway line; we could hear, less than ten metres behind us the bursts of submachine guns, the grenade explosions and the flares going off over our heads. I tried to give us some breathing space with my Colt pistol but I had a malfunction after firing four rounds. Pistol in hand, we then reached the big wall which separated the "Secours National" park from another estate which bordered the Aulnay marshalling yard. The three of us tried to go over that bridge; after two unsuccesful tries, I told the two FFIs it was useless to keep on trying at this location and that I would try to go over that wall somewhere else. They kept on trying and that was the last I ever saw of them.

I finally managed to go over that wall 20 metres away, then went over another fence which took me to the streets and railway lines. Another group of Boche which was located near the railway lines saw me and opened up with their submachine guns; even though they probably were only about ten metres from me, they missed. I went into the marshalling yard which was guarded by another German patrol which had nothing to do with the unit which had ambushed us. On seeing me, they shouted some warnings then opened up again on me with their submachine guns at very close range, missing me yet again. I went across all the railways, going over another fence which took me to a road which bordered the train station. Another pair of Boche with submachine guns was there and they also shouted warnings before firing at me; luckily, I tripped as I went over the fence which meant I fell behind a concrete parapet which protected me from the bursts. Understanding the magazines of their submachine guns were empty, I ran to the neighbouring houses. After two or three hundred metres of a very uncomfortable run as I was wounded both in my toe, hand and left kneecap and had multiple bruises, I saw a house with an open gate and entered it. I ran into a woman who, on seeing my arrival meant trouble, told me: "Don't come in, run away, get out of here". I threatened her with my pistol and told her to "shut up" and ran to the fourth floor using the back staircase. Exhausted, I slid down the wall and sat in front of an apartment door; I was later to learnt this was the flat of a Gestapo female informant ! I was to remain there for the rest of the night, my Colt pistol in one hand and a cyanide pill in the other, ready to use both if I was to do a last stand. The searches went on all night in the area, all houses being raided by the Germans except the one where I was hiding…

Around 0545 hours, as day broke, I went down the stairs, determi-

*Opposite.*
**Battery transit box and Willard battery used to power the Paraset (or Mark 7) of Pierre Ravarre during the "Montre" mission in the city of Montbéliard in September 1944.**
*(Sussex picture collection)*

58

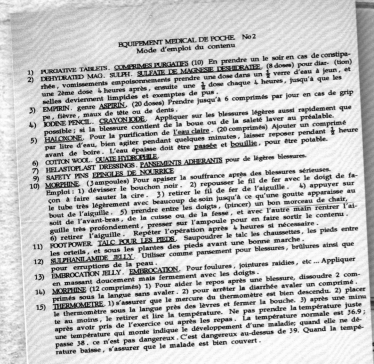

EQUIPEMENT MEDICAL DE POCHE. No 2
Mode d'emploi du contenu

1) PURGATIVE TABLETS. COMPRIMES PURGATIFS (10) En prendre un le soir en cas de constipa-
2) DEHYDRATED MAG. SULPH. SULFATE DE MAGNESIE DESHIDRATEE. (8 doses) pour diar- (tion)
rhée, vomissements empoisonnements prendre une dose dans un ½ verre d'eau à jeun, et
une 2ème dose 4 heures après, ensuite une ¼ dose chaque 4 heures, jusqu'à que les
selles deviennent limpides et exemptes de pus.
3) EMPIRIN. genre ASPIRIN. (20 doses) Prendre jusqu'à 6 comprimés par jour en cas de grip
pe, fièvre, maux de tête ou de dents.
4) IODINE PENCIL. CRAYON IODE. Appliquer sur les blessures légères aussi rapidement que
possible ; si la blessure contient de la boue ou de la saleté laver au préalable.
5) HALOXONE. Pour la purification de l'eau claire. (20 comprimés) Ajouter un comprimé
par litre d'eau, bien agiter pendant quelques minutes, laisser reposer pendant ½ heure
avant de boire. L'eau épaisse doit être passée et bouillie, pour être potable.
6) COTTON WOOL. OUATE HYDROPHILE.
7) HELASTOPLAST DRESSINGS. PANSEMENTS ADHERANTS pour de légères blessures.
9) SAFETY PINS EPINGLES DE NOURRICE
10) MORPHINE. (3 ampoules) Pour apaiser la souffrance après des blessures sérieuses.
Emploi : 1) dévisser le bouchon noir. 2) repousser le fil de fer avec le doigt de fa-
çon à faire sauter la cire. 3) retirer le fil de fer de l'aiguille. 4) appuyer sur
le tube très légèrement avec beaucoup de soin jusqu'à ce qu'une goutte apparaisse au
bout de l'aiguille. 5) prendre entre les doigts, (pincer) un bon morceau de chair,
soit de l'avant-bras, de la cuisse ou de la fesse, et avec l'autre main rentrer l'aiguille très profondement, presser sur l'ampoule pour en faire sortir le contenu.
6) retirer l'aiguille. Répéter l'opération après 4 heures si nécessaire.
11) FOOTPOWER. TALC POUR LES PIEDS. Saupoudrer le talc les chaussettes, les pieds entre
les orteils, et sous les plantes des pieds avant une bonne marche.
12) SULPHANILAMIDE JELLY. Utiliser comme pansement pour blessures, brûlures ainsi que
pour erruptions de la peau.
13) EMBROCATION JELLY. EMBROCATION. Pour foulures, jointures raidies, etc... Appliquer
en massant doucement mais fermement avec les doigts.
14) MORPHINE (12 comprimés) 1) Pour aider le repos après une blessure, dissoudre 2 comprimés sous la langue sans avaler. 2) pour arrêter la diarrhée avaler un comprimé.
15) THERMOMETRE. 1) s'assurer que le mercure du thermomètre est bien descendu. 2) placer
le thermomètre sous la langue près des lèvres et fermer la bouche. 3) après une minu
te au moins, le retirer et lire la température. Ne pas prendre la température juste
après avoir pris de l'exercice ou après les repas. La température normale est 36.9 ;
une température qui monte indique le développement d'une maladie; quand elle ne dé-
passe 38. ce n'est pas dangereux. C'est dangereux au-dessus de 39. Quand la température baisse, s'assurer que le malade est bien couvert.

ned to ask the first French male civilian I would meet help. A man, the name of whom I never learnt, took me to his flat, allowed me to clean myself up, gave me a pair of canvas loafer and a donkey jacket and, on my request, met up with Mr. Savaut who lived nearby to organise my extraction. Ten minutes later, Mrs. Savaut parked her Citroën "Traction avant" in front of the house; I slid in the back seat and we left Aulnay without any problem even though German patrols were still active in the area. I then asked Mrs. Savaut to drive me to the city of Drancy, where I would meet Mrs. Poileux I had known for a long time and to then warn Chaloner whose safe house was a mere 500 metres from where the shoot-out had occurred the previous nigt. She very bravely carried out both tasks.

When in Drancy, I asked Germaine Poileux to warn all my Livry safe houses of what had happened so they could get ready for possible German searches since I had had to abandon a jacket with my forged ID documents during the shoot-out. There was no other incriminating document in that jacket except the hand-written address of commandant Ledron in Champigny-sur-Marne. Chaloner had him warned the very same morning by a bicycle mounted courier.

I also asked Jacques Girard to send me a medical doctor who knew nothing of my activities and background.

Doctor Mesplomb came a few hours later and treated my wounds. He then found a safe house for me in Le Raincy, at Mrs. Clavaus, the head of a boarding school for mentally retarded children. In this way, I managed to escape the Gestapo.

I was later to learn that the two young FFIs who had acted as my protection detail on that night were shot after having been savagely tortured. They did not speak.

It is also my duty to mention the courageous behaviour of Mrs. Marie Debrin, Dr Perlis' house maid who remained in the house for the duration of the events, never gave the Germans any valuable information and did everything she could to try and save the lives of the two young FFIs.

Above.
*Medical Kit and its operating manual. Each agent who was parachuted inside occupied France received one of those kits, which fitted in a dedicated pocket of the SOE jumpsuit. Among other items, this kit held three morphine syringes, some field dressings and water purification tablets.*
(Sussex picture collection)

*Opposite.*
**Lieutenant René's a.k.a "Chaloner", a.k.a "Ducasse" French and British ID Cards.**

*Below.*
**Georges Ducasse's Distinguished Service Cross.**
*(Sussex collection pictures)*

DISTINGUISHED
SERVICE CROSS

# THE "VITRAIL" MISSION

Opposite.
**Lieutenant Jacques Voyer a.k.a "Lucien", an observer in of the "Vitrail" mission. He was arrested and wounded on 10 June 1944 during a close target reconnaissance and then interrogated and tortured until the 27 of June. On that date he was executed in the bois de Chavannes near Chartres. He was made a posthumous Compagnon de la Libération.**
*(Musée de l'Ordre de la Libération picture/collection Sussex)*

---

**Parachuted during the night of 10 to 11 April 1944 in Le Blanc (200 km from Chartres in the Indre département)**
Area of operation: Chartres
Captain Jacques Voyer a.k.a "Lucien Voyer" (observer)
Lieutenant André Guillebaud a.k.a "André Lebaud"
(radio operator)

Parachuted during the night of 10 to 11 April 1944, Jacques Voyer (observer) and André Guillebaud (radio operator) had the Chartres region as their area of operation. They also received two parachute drops of men and equipment. Their operational results were very satisfactory and they radioed back a large quantity of highly valuable intelligence reports, particularly on the movements of the "Panzer- Lehr" armoured division.

On one occasion, while on a "road watch" mission, André Guillebaud noticed some unknown tactical markings on different vehicles. He quickly reproduced them on a sketch and then gave them to Jacques Voyer in the hope he could recognise them. On 10 June, as Voyer had gotten closer to the convoy in order to gather better intelligence, he was arrested by two Feldgendarmen who asked him to show his ID. While checking on him, the German found the sketches with the tactical markings; Voyer then tried to escape but he was hit by two bullets and immediately detained. Tortured during eight days, he did not speak. On 26 June, he was sentenced to death for espionage by a military tribunal. He was shot the very next day on the Chavannes shooting range near Chartres. On 20 January 1946, General de Gaulle made him a posthumous Compagnon de la Libération while the American authorities awarded him the Distinguished Service Cross. André Guillebaud managed to escape the Germans and carried out another operation in the North of France. He also received the Distinguished Service Cross from the American authorities.

*Opposite.*
**Lieutenant André Guillebaud a.k.a "Lebeau", Jacques Voyer's radio operator. He eventually linked up with another Sussex team near Amiens and carried out a second mission.**
*(Sussex picture collection)*

*Opposite.*
**Capitaine Pierre Vergès d'Espagne's signet ring. It had a hidden compartment in which to hide a cyanide pill. Another type of ring was also used to hide a tiny compass.**
*(Sussex picture collection)*

*Opposite.*
**Coding pad printed on silk used by the "Vitrail" team which operated in the city of Chartres.**
*(Sussex collection picture)*

*Next page.*
**Extremely rare picture of the "Drolot" Sussex team at work : Lieutenants Brochard and Lart sending a report with a British Mark 7 radio set from a garage located in the city of Amiens.**
*(Sussex collection picture)*

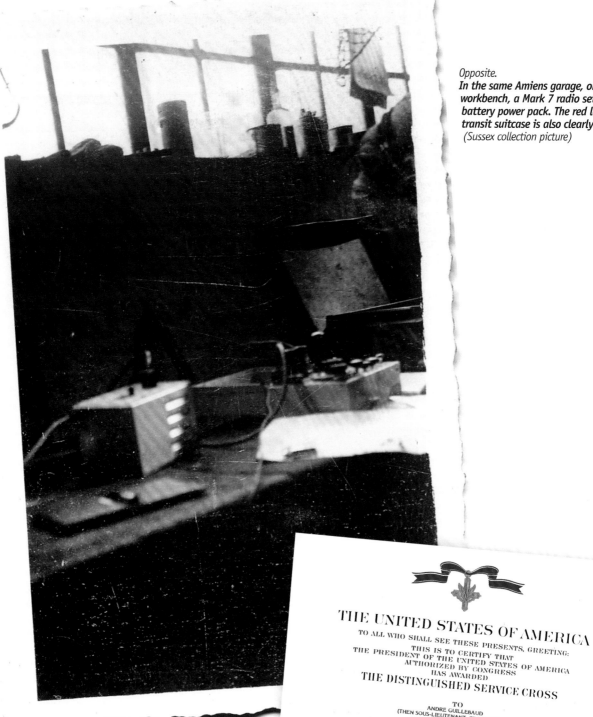

*Opposite.*
**In the same Amiens garage, on the workbench, a Mark 7 radio set and its battery power pack. The red leather transit suitcase is also clearly visible.**
*(Sussex collection picture)*

*Opposite.*
**The certificate of the American Distinguished Service Cross awarded to André Guillebaud by the United States' Government for his gallant conduct during the "Vitrail" mission.**
*(Sussex collection picture)*

# THE UNITED STATES OF AMERICA

TO ALL WHO SHALL SEE THESE PRESENTS, GREETING:

THIS IS TO CERTIFY THAT
THE PRESIDENT OF THE UNITED STATES OF AMERICA
AUTHORIZED BY CONGRESS
HAS AWARDED

## THE DISTINGUISHED SERVICE CROSS

TO
ANDRE GUILLEBAUD
(THEN SOUS-LIEUTENANT, FRENCH ARMY)
FOR
**EXTRAORDINARY HEROISM IN ACTION**

IN FRANCE FROM 10 APRIL 1944 TO 27 JUNE 1944

GIVEN UNDER MY HAND IN THE CITY OF WASHINGTON
THIS        24TH        DAY OF        JULY        19 91

THE ADJUTANT GENERAL

SECRETARY OF THE ARMY

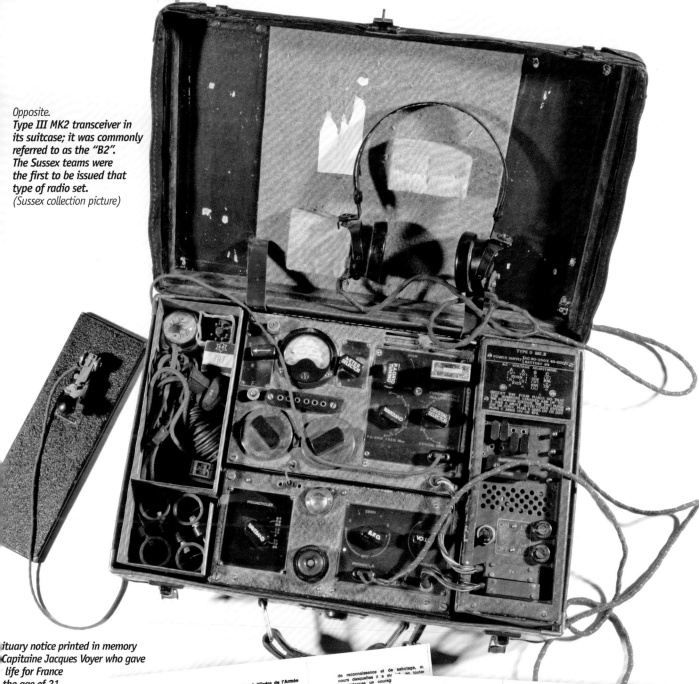

*Opposite.*
**Type III MK2 transceiver in its suitcase; it was commonly referred to as the "B2". The Sussex teams were the first to be issued that type of radio set.**
*(Sussex collection picture)*

...ituary notice printed in memory ...Capitaine Jacques Voyer who gave ...life for France ...the age of 21. ...services were also ...ognized by the United ...tes' Government ...ich awarded him the ...tinguished Service ...ss "for extraordinary ...roism in connection ...th military operations ...ainst an armed enemy, ...action against enemy ...ces on April ...- June 27, 1944".
...ussex collection picture)

*Opposite.*
**Lieutenant Georges Soulier "Gérard Boudemange", a.k.a "Georges Sautel", a.k.a "Alain Wallon", a.k.a "Jacques Beauzac", wearing an American uniform. This picture was taken in London in September 1944 between two missions.**
*(Sussex collection picture)*

# THE "VIS" MISSION

BCRA, OSSEX

The bearer of this card whose photograph and signature appear hereon, is attached to the United States Armed Forces and is on active duty. Any assistance given him in the performance of his duties will be appreciated. Any inquiries should be directed to the undersigned.

Le porteur de la présente carte, dont la photographie et la signature sont apposées ci-dessus, est attaché à l'Armée des Etats-Unis et est en service actif. Toute assistance qui lui sera donnée dans l'accomplissement de sa mission sera hautement appreciée. Toutes demandes de renseignements complémentaires doivent être addressees au soussigné.

Valid until 31 Déc. '44
Valable jusqu'au

s/Lt. BOUDEMANGE, Gerard
*(Signature of Bearer)*

1st Lt. William B. Boyd
*(Official Signature)*
Hq. Com. Z (FWD)
Date 19 October 1944

## Extract from the memories of Georges Soulier

AFTER HAVING SETTLED IN BLOIS, Jourdet took the habit of having all his meals in restaurants. One evening, he had a brief clash with the head of the local Vichy Milice whom attention he had attracted. The city's police superintendent then warned Jourdet that he had received orders to arrest him the next morning; he thus had to leave town immediately. He came to see me at la Chapelle-Vendômoise, told me in a few words

*Opposite.*
**OSS identification document belonging to Georges Soulier. This document allowed its bearer to move around freely during a mission and proved Soulier belonged to the US armed forces.**
*(Sussex collection picture)*

what had happened and informed me that his plan was now to seek shelter with some relatives in Roanne; he gave me the address and then left at once. The same evening, on my scheduled broadcast to London, I reported the incident as well as the departure of Jourdet. I then proposed to pursue the mission on my own since with my network of informants, I was in a position to answer all the intelligence requests they could have thrown at me. London's answer was of course positive and they thanked me profusely while at the same time insisting on the fact that I was not to take any unnecessary risks. I thus continued the mission. Meanwhile, all sorts of information kept on reaching me and the duration of my radio broadcasts kept on increasing. All this was of course in direct contradiction to all the safety measures we had learnt in training, but what else was I suppose to do? And of course, I ended up being "D.F'd" (located by radio direction finding devices) by the Germans. At that stage I need to explain how direction finding worked, or more precisely how it worked at the time.

This was what we called triangulation; we had received classes on it in Saint Albans. We knew there were three main DF centres in France. By combining the direction information from those three suitably spaced receivers, the source of a transmission could be located in space via triangulation; the three lines created a triangle of variable size. A plane was then sent over that area in order to narrow down the area of interest. That plane was easy to identify as it was fitted with several antennas and flew at a low altitude. Once the area from which the emitter was operating was suitably pinpointed, a van was then used. Its role was given away by the fact that most of its bodywork was made of wood in order to limit electromagnetic interferences. Inside the van, hidden from views, a signal intelligence specialist followed the clandestine broadcasts through a headset until he could direct the vehicle to the exact location of the radio operator. Most of the time, the vehicle was disguised as a department store delivery van; when it had reached the immediate vicinity of the clandestine broadcast, the DF van had

*Above.*
**Lieutenant Henri Jourdet a.k.a "Henri Waas", the observer of the "Vis" mission.**
*(Sussex collection picture)*

*Opposite.*
**QB (Quick Burn) paper sheets. Sussex agents were issued note pads made of QB ; being partially made of powder, this paper self destroyed immediately when touched by the tip of a lit cigarette. Standard operating procedures enforced the use of QB paper when encoding and decoding messages.**
*(Sussex collection picture)*

*Above.*
**The crew of the 406 Bomb Squadron B-24 Liberator which dropped the "Vis" Sussex team during the night of the 1st to the 2nd of June 1944. Standing, left to right: Clinton Rabbit (pilot), Ernest Asbury (co-pilot), Floyd Olson (navigator), Donald Leinhauser (bomber). Kneeling, left to right: Nick Rasnack (dispatcher), Steve Sianis (radio operator), Mike Tauger (tail gunner) and Art Bogusz (flight engineer).**
*(Sussex collection picture)*

*Above.*
**B-24 Liberator "Brer-Rabbit" of 406th Bomb Squadron of the "Carpetbaggers" revving up its engine on the tarmac of the Harrington Air Base.**
*(Sussex collection picture)*

The "Vis" missions were over. During the liberation of the city of Blois, Captain Alden of the OSS picks up Georges Soulier who is visible on the right of the picture as well as Jacques Coulon (standing in the back of the Jeep) who belonged to the "Foudre" mission.
(Sussex collection picture)

*Opposite.*
**Forged identity card used by Georges Soulier in the name of "Georges Sautel".** This document was used during the "Vis" mission in Blois.
(Sussex collection picture)

*Opposite.*
**Georges Soulier's Allied Military Identity Card in the name of "Gérard Boudemange".**
(Sussex collection picture)

to go very slowly. It was not uncommon for German signal intelligence specialists to pretend their vehicle had broken down in order to slowly push it by hand without drawing too much attention. When the DF teams had reached that point, the radio operator had better get the hell out of dodge; unfortunately, too often, the operators were so engrossed in their broadcasts that they never saw the DF teams until it was too late.

As I said before, an 11-year old girl was living in the farm. Since it was summertime, she was on holidays. Her father, monsieur Ouzilleau, had told her never ever to mention my presence to anybody outside the immediate family circle. She had understood it was very important. She was a nice girl, a little bit wild and she was always playing on her own outside, in front of the farm. When I was broadcasting, I had

*Close up on the right pocket of Georges Soulier's US Army walking out uniform on which the ribbons of the croix de guerre 1939-1945 with one citation and American Silver Star. The often seen Free French badge worn underneath the ribbon bar was called the "Mosquito» by the fighting French. (Sussex collection picture)*

*Opposite.*
**Presentation box holding Georges Soulier's individually named Silver Star, a reduced size ribbon bar for civilian wear and a uniform-size ribbon bar.**
*(Sussex collection picture)*

*Below.*
**Sous-lieutenant Georges Soulier's Silver Star certificate awarded for "Gallantry in action" during the "Vis" mission.**
*(Sussex collection picture)*

THE UNITED STATES OF AMERICA

TO ALL WHO SHALL SEE THESE PRESENTS, GREETING:

THIS IS TO CERTIFY THAT
THE PRESIDENT OF THE UNITED STATES OF AMERICA
AUTHORIZED BY ACT OF CONGRESS JULY 9, 1918
HAS AWARDED

THE SILVER STAR

TO

GEORGES SOULIER
(THEN SOUS-LIEUTENANT, FRENCH ARMY)
FOR
GALLANTRY IN ACTION
IN FRANCE FROM 2 JUNE 1944 TO 18 AUGUST 1944
GIVEN UNDER MY HAND IN THE CITY OF WASHINGTON
THIS 20th DAY OF DECEMBER 19 91

THE ADJUTANT GENERAL                    SECRETARY OF THE ARMY

DA FORM 4980-4, APR 81

RESTRICTED

(GO 49, 1 Apr 1945, contd)

Despite a lack of any pre-arranged organization, he built a strong intelligence network at Alencon and dispatched significant tactical intelligence on enemy units, command posts, depots, and motor parks. At his request, he was parachuted into France a second time because his first mission was curtailed by the speed of the allied advance. In the five days before he was over-run by the allied advance, he contrived to gather and transmit intelligence on enemy positions and movements to London headquarters and to the United States Seventh Army.

Sous-Lieutenant Georges Soulier, French Army, for gallantry in action behind the enemy lines from 2 June 1944 to 18 August 1944. Sous-Lieutenant Soulier was parachuted into France in civilian clothes, together with a team-mate, as a radio operator for a secret intelligence team in Blois. He worked with his team-mate until it became necessary for the latter to move to avoid being captured. He then carried on alone, collecting and transmitting very good intelligence reports. Twice he was detected and had to change his location to elude capture. Sous-Lieutenant Soulier's courage, ingenuity, and resourcefulness resulted in the successful accomplishment of his intelligence mission.

Sous-Lieutenant Jacques Suissa, French Army, for gallantry in action behind the enemy lines from 12 July 1944 to 15 October 1944. Sous-Lieutenant Suissa was parachuted into France in civilian clothes as a secret intelligence agent. Acting as an organizer of an intelligence network and as his own radio operator he transmitted intelligence concerning all the bridges of the Indre and Creuse rivers, troop movements, strength of armament, air raid results, and enemy identifications. While the chief of the mission was away in the Limoges area, he took over the responsibilities of two other networks. Despite his youth, he proved to have organizational ability, initiative and leadership and often undertook great risks in gathering information.

Sous-Lieutenant Henri L. Vergon, French Army, for gallantry in action behind the enemy lines from 9 April 1944 to 8 August 1944. Sous-Lieutenant Vergon was parachuted into France in civilian clothes as a radio operator for a secret intelligence team. He and his observer established themselves in Le Mans, organized a complete network of informants. When his observer was arrested, he withdrew to his emergency hide-out and attempted to make emergency contact with his emergency radio set. He failed in his attempts to make contact, so he returned to Le Mans and participated in the liberation of the city. Through his ingenuity and resourcefulness, he eluded detection and successfully carried out his intelligence mission.

BY COMMAND OF GENERAL EISENHOWER:

OFFICIAL:
                                        R. B. LORD,
                                        Major General, GSC, Deputy Chief of Staff.

R. B. LOVETT,
Brigadier General, USA, Adjutant General.

DISTRIBUTION: E

*Above.*
**Citations signed by General Eisenhower and dated 1 April 1945 on which Georges Soulier and Henri Vergon of the Sussex plan as well as Jacques Suissa of the Proust plan are mentioned.**
*(Sussex collection picture)*

asked her to keep a good watch on the surroundings and to immediately report any activity, especially the movement of vehicles, as soon as she had spotted them. One has to remember that traffic was then very light compared to today and cars were not a common sight, especially in the countryside. One evening, I was transmitting a very long message when she suddenly arrived in a hurry; she reported that there was a slow moving car on the road, still some distance from our position; I quickly checked through the window and there it was, a DF van being slowly pushed by two men. Without a doubt, they were on the last phase of their direction finding effort. I lost no time to hide all my equipment and remove all traces of my presence in the farm. For added safety, I left through the back door and hid in a nearby wheat field. Once danger was gone, I returned to the farm; nobody had been threatened or hurt. This time, it had been a close call and I knew I owed a huge debt of gratitude to the little girl; she had saved my life.

Of course, I could no longer broadcast from that location.

As always, when I had arrived in that area, I had looked for a secondary safe house. Martel had found a good place for me, at some friends, in Onzain, 15 km Sout West from the city of Blois, on the river Loire. As soon as I had returned to the farm, I had Martel warned in order for him to come, pick me up and bring me to

Onzain. He did just that the next morning. On the road, he warned me that monsieur Sibenaler was the manager of quite a big wood cutting factory and that he was, among other contracts, in charge of providing wooden boards for the provisional repairs of the bridges that allied air raids and sabotage operations had destroyed. As a consequence, he often had to receive German officers in his office but I needn't worry, he was a trusted friend. I was thus introduced to him and Martel then returned to work.

Monsieur Sibenaler made me very welcome. We sat under a tree, in the garden and he then poured me a glass of a nice Anjou wine. I had dropped my suitcase radio and my spare battery on the ground, next to me. We were chatting away when suddenly a German officer arrived. Monsieur Sibenaler reassured me; this man was one of his customers. He quickly threw a canvas sack over my equipment, introduced me as a friend and invited the officer to seat next to me. I was not feeling good at all but in the end, all went well. We drank together and then the German left after having sorted a few things out with Sibenaler; in fact, they were finalising a wooden boards order to repair the Blois railway bridge I had organised the bombing off

Opposite.
On returning to London after their operational missions and as a special privilege, the "Sussex" agents who had operated for the American Ossex missions were allowed to wear the official US Army walking out uniform. Those uniforms were generally purchased in a PX. The picture shows Georges Soulier's uniform composed of the chocolate brown jacket and service cap and "Pink" trousers. The only French elements of this uniform are the Free French parachute wings and insignia, the France shoulder titles, the Sussex insignia, the shoulder rank slides and a decoration.
(Sussex collection picture)

*Above.*

**On that picture taken on the occasion of the liberation of the city of Blois, some of the agents locally recruited during the "Vis" mission can be identified. Left to right : Colonel Fremiot, monsieur Martel, Maurice Fleury, Georges Soulier, mademoiselle Sibenaler (holding a puppy), an unidentified woman, madame Sibenaler, Hélène Jourdain, monsieur Sibenaler.**

*(Sussex collection picture)*

previously. I have to admit I started relaxing once he had departed.

I now had to find a new secondary safe house. Monsieur Sibenaler told me he had a little fishing cabin on the other side of the river Loire, on the banks of the river Beuvron, a small tributary of the Loire, no more than ten kilometres from Onzain, near a hamlet named "Les Montils". He had a small dinghy there so I could cross the river and he told me he would put a bicycle on the other side so I could reach the cabin.

I thus started working hard again, especially since Maurice Fleury kept on bringing me highly valuable intelligence. On one occasion, he spotted a large concentration of German lorries near his parents' home; he gave me the grid coordinates and I immediately passed the report to London. On the same evening, three American bombers did a bombing run; unfortunately, they missed their target and the bombs landed close to Maurice's house but neither him nor his house were hit.

During the same period, Martel asked him to report the location of a large German convoy made up of a minimum of 25 tanks and as many supporting vehicles. They were resting while on their way to the Normandy front. Once again, I reported the coordinate to London. This time, the bombers did not miss their targets and the next day it was possible to still see many smouldering wrecks of metal where the convoy had been. Everything went perfectly during the first two weeks but one day, as I had just completed a broadcast, I heard the sound of a plane my headset I prevented me from hearing. I looked up and saw a DF plane circling over Onzain. I did not need any other warning! This time, I did not wait for the arrival of the DF van. I crossed the Loire with the dinghy, got on my bike and reached the fishing cabin in which I settled. Once there, it immediately appeared to me that this could only be a temporary solution; I was now far from everything and getting in contact with my liaison elements and runners had become quite complicated. Thus, when Maurice Fleury offered to accommodate me at his place, I gladly accepted his offer while keeping the fishing cabin as an emergency location since I had never been spotted while there.

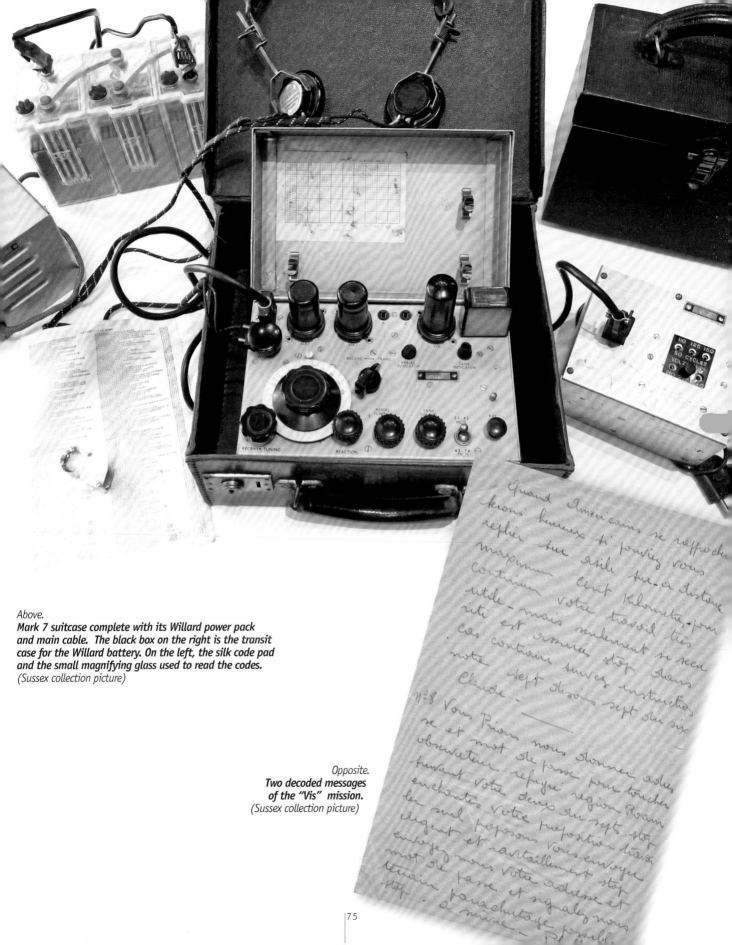

*Above.*
**Mark 7 suitcase complete with its Willard power pack and main cable. The black box on the right is the transit case for the Willard battery. On the left, the silk code pad and the small magnifying glass used to read the codes.**
*(Sussex collection picture)*

*Opposite.*
**Two decoded messages of the "Vis" mission.**
*(Sussex collection picture)*

I settled at Maurice's who lived with his parents at Villebarou, a small hamlet near Blois. I kept on operating but the month of August had arrived and the American forces were near. I then received a message ordering me to establish contact with a certain "Captain Beau" from the American G2 (the military intelligence branch) as soon as the first American forces were to reach Blois. The next day, Blois was liberated….an explosion of joy !

I quickly found Captain Beau and introduced myself. He asked me whether it would be possible, once I had left, to set up teams that would keep on providing intelligence reports on what was happening on the other side of the Loire between Blois and Tours where the Germans had now retreated. I promised I would do my best. With the help of Martel and Fleury, I established contact with the Blois, Onzain, Amboise and Tours FFI groups.

Various teams were deployed and they kept on going back and forth over the Loire; the intelligence reports were collected by Fleury who in turn gave them to the G2 and Captain Beau.

A few days after the area had been liberated, I had the pleasure of welcoming Captain Saint Clair; he had come to pick me up in a Jeep and was in the company of "Olivier" whose real name was in fact Jacques Coulon. I had trained with him whilst in Saint Albans. Originating from the area, he had asked Saint Clair whether he could come along with him since he was hoping to see his parents who lived in Amboise. Together with Martel, Fleury and Sibenaler, we had a memorable lunch in a Onzain restaurant in order to celebrate the liberation and us getting together again. It was then time to leave the region. With Saint Clair and Coulon we took a Jeep to Paris, which had been liberated a few days before. During the trip, Saint Clair congratulated me for the work I had done; he told me the Allied high command had been very satisfied with

the reports I had sent. I was very happy to hear all that. It was also during that trip that I learnt of the arrest of many friends, particularly of the "Colère", "Salaud" and "Filan" teams. Those arrests had taken place in Vendôme, not that far from my area of operations. On the road, we overtook many military convoys and in each town, people were packing the sidewalks to see us drive by and to cheer and applaud us. In one of those towns where we had stopped for a minute, and old man begged us to come to his place and share a glass in honour of victory with him. He produced an old bottle of white wine he had saved for a very special occasion during countless years; religiously, he opened it and filled some glasses but the wine was so old that it had turned into a kind of thick syrup with a foul taste…but this man looked so happy to offer us this bottle that we finally found the strength to drink it. We arrived in Paris on 1 September. My mission was over!

**BCRA, OSSEX**

# THE "MADELEINE" MISSION

Opposite.
**ID sketch, drawn by Thoorens, of commandant André Lefebvre a.k.a "Ledron", the observer of the "Madeleine" mission.**
(Sussex collection picture)

Parachuted on 1st June 1944 on the Savennières racetrack west of the city of Angers (Maine-et-Loire département)

Area of operation: city of Vincennes
End of mission: 27 August 1944
Major André Lefebvre a.k.a "Alfred Ledron" (observer)
Lieutenant Daniel Pomeranz a.k.a "Daniel Piron" (radio operator)

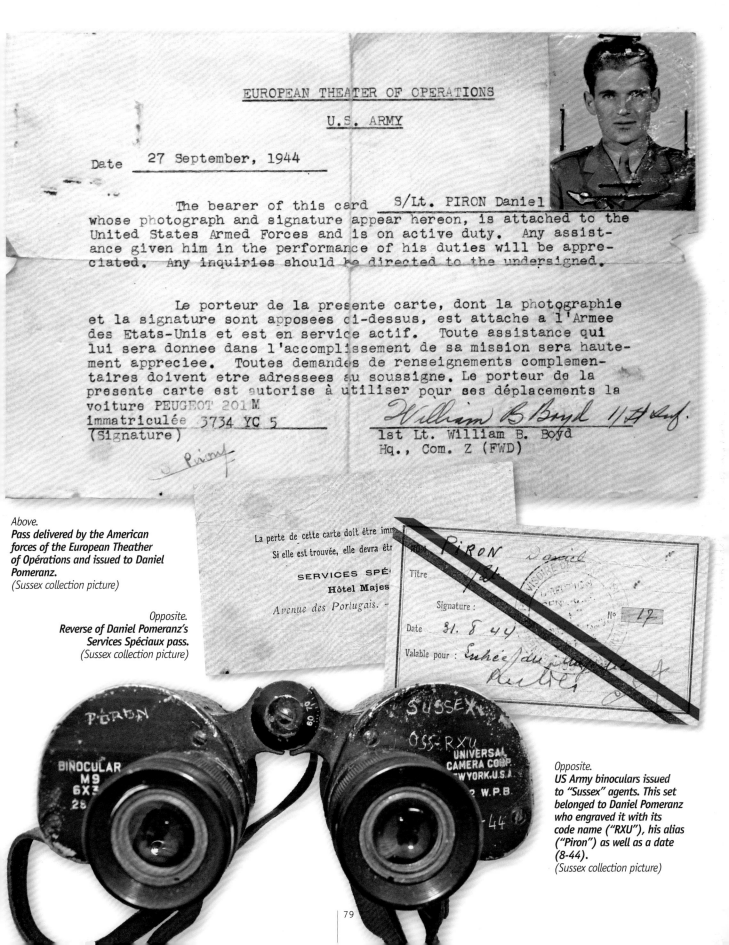

EUROPEAN THEATER OF OPERATIONS

U.S. ARMY

Date   27 September, 1944

The bearer of this card   S/Lt. PIRON Daniel whose photograph and signature appear hereon, is attached to the United States Armed Forces and is on active duty. Any assistance given him in the performance of his duties will be appreciated. Any inquiries should be directed to the undersigned.

Le porteur de la presente carte, dont la photographie et la signature sont apposees ci-dessus, est attache a l'Armee des Etats-Unis et est en service actif. Toute assistance qui lui sera donnee dans l'accomplissement de sa mission sera hautement appreciee. Toutes demandes de renseignements complementaires doivent etre adressees au soussigne. Le porteur de la presente carte est autorise à utiliser pour ses déplacements la voiture PEUGEOT 201 M immatriculée 3734 YC 5
(Signature)

1st Lt. William B. Boyd
Hq., Com. Z (FWD)

*Above.*
**Pass delivered by the American forces of the European Theather of Opérations and issued to Daniel Pomeranz.**
*(Sussex collection picture)*

*Opposite.*
**Reverse of Daniel Pomeranz's Services Spéciaux pass.**
*(Sussex collection picture)*

La perte de cette carte doit être imm
Si elle est trouvée, elle devra êtr

SERVICES SPÉC
Hôtel Majes
Avenue des Portugais. –

NOM  PIRON  Daniel
Titre
Signature :
Date  31. 8 44
Valable pour :

*Opposite.*
**US Army binoculars issued to "Sussex" agents. This set belonged to Daniel Pomeranz who engraved it with its code name ("RXU"), his alias ("Piron") as well as a date (8-44).**
*(Sussex collection picture)*

*Opposite.*
**Daniel Pomeranz's decorations showing service during both World War two and the war in Algeria : Légion d'Honneur, Croix de Guerre with one citation, Croix de la Valeur Militaire with three citations, Croix des engagés volontaire, médaille commémorative 39-45, médaille commémorative Algérie, American Bronze Star.**
*(Sussex collection picture)*

*Opposite.*
**Daniel Pomeranz's B2 dagger. He used it during the "Madeleine" mission.**
*(Sussex collection picture)*

*Opposite.*
*An AMK III radio suitcase and operating manual. This set was used as a back-up system by Pomeranz during the "Madeleine" mission.*
*(Sussex collection)*

*Opposite.*
*Canvas travel bags issued to all "Sussex" agents. When the "Vis", "Madeleine", "Marbot" and "Cure", "Sussex" teams were all dropped during the same night on the same DZ and all ended up on the same train platform the next morning, there was a total of eight agents at the same location all carrying the same travel bag ! It was not exactly considered a discreet start of a mission…*
*(Sussex collection picture)*

*Below.*
**Lieutenant Daniel Pomeranz during the "Madeleine" mission.**
*(Sussex collection picture)*

*Above.*
**British Parachute Regiment beret badge minus its crown as worn by Free French paratroopers, France shoulder titles (large type) and Free French parachute wings belonging to Daniel Pomeranz.**
*(Sussex collection picture)*

*Next page.*
**Daniel Pomeranz a.k.a "Piron", the "Madeleine" mission radio operator. His mobility depended on a bicycle during most of his mission. The suitcase of the Mark 7 transmitter can be clearly seen on the luggage rack of his bicycle.**
*(Sussex collection picture)*

*Below.*
**Daniel Pomeranz metal "dog tags".**
*(Sussex collection picture)*

Parachuted during the night of 7 to 8 June 1944 in La Ferté Alais (Essonne département)

Area of operation: Vaire-sur-Marne and its region
End of mission: 1 September 1944
Lieutenant Robert Pissier a.k.a "Max Verneuil" (observer)
Lieutenant Henri Tosi a.k.a "Henri Bousquet" (radio operator)

*Opposite.*
*Lieutenant Henri Tosi a.k.a "Bousquet",*
*the "Cendrillon" mission radio operator. Henri Tosi wears*
*an M1 Field Jacket with Second Lieutenant rank slides,*
*Free French parachute wings, Sussex insignia #44 and*
*either silver or gold metal France shoulder titles.*
*(Sussex collection picture)*

# THE "CENDRILLON" MISSION

BCRA, OSSEX

*Opposite.*
*A N°69 "Striker" grenade made of bakelite. Each agent had two such grenades tucked in its jumpsuit when inserting into occupied France. The operating principle was identical to the N°82 "Gammon"; both only exploded on contact, not on a delay.*
*(Sussex collection)*

*Opposite.*
**Henri Tosi's forged ID.**
*(Sussex collection picture)*

*Above.*
**A "Défense Passive" (civilian protection service) Ausweis (German-issued pass) in the name of "Pariset", Henri Tosi's alias during his first mission.**
*(Sussex collection picture)*

*Opposite.*
**Henri Tosi's radio logbook with main and secondary frequencies and a summary of security measures.**
*(Sussex collection picture)*

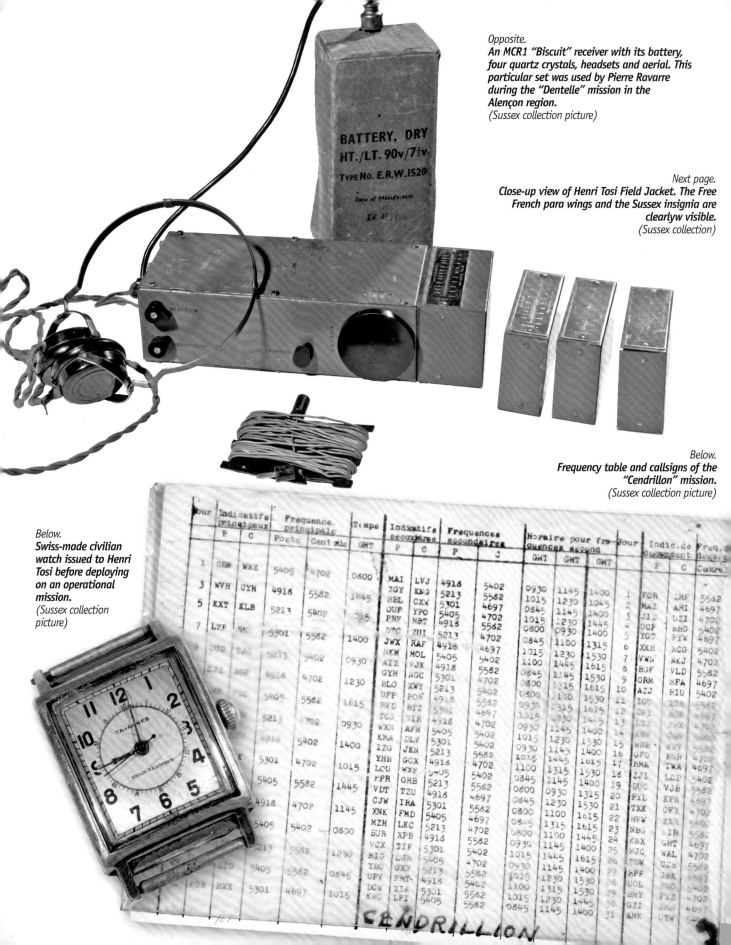

*Opposite.*
**An MCR1 "Biscuit" receiver with its battery, four quartz crystals, headsets and aerial. This particular set was used by Pierre Ravarre during the "Dentelle" mission in the Alençon region.**
*(Sussex collection picture)*

*Next page.*
**Close-up view of Henri Tosi Field Jacket. The Free French para wings and the Sussex insignia are clearlyw visible.**
*(Sussex collection)*

*Below.*
**Frequency table and callsigns of the "Cendrillon" mission.**
*(Sussex collection picture)*

*Below.*
**Swiss-made civilian watch issued to Henri Tosi before deploying on an operational mission.**
*(Sussex collection picture)*

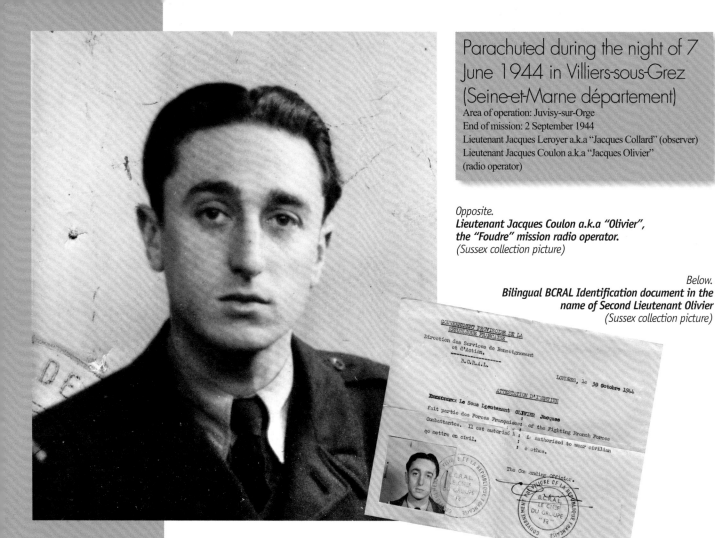

Parachuted during the night of 7 June 1944 in Villiers-sous-Grez (Seine-et-Marne département)

Area of operation: Juvisy-sur-Orge
End of mission: 2 September 1944
Lieutenant Jacques Leroyer a.k.a "Jacques Collard" (observer)
Lieutenant Jacques Coulon a.k.a "Jacques Olivier" (radio operator)

*Opposite.*
**Lieutenant Jacques Coulon a.k.a "Olivier", the "Foudre" mission radio operator.**
*(Sussex collection picture)*

*Below.*
**Bilingual BCRAL Identification document in the name of Second Lieutenant Olivier**
*(Sussex collection picture)*

# THE "FOUDRE" MISSION

BCRA, OSSEX

*Top right.*
**Jacques Coulon's ribbon bar: Croix de Guerre 1939-1945 with one citation and American Bronze Star. Underneath is a small version of the Free French Naval Forces (FNFL) insignia which was nicknamed "the coffin" because of its shape.**
*(Sussex collection)*

*Opposite.*
**Close up on the bullion "France" shoulder title sewn on the US Army issue walking out jacket of Jacques Coulon.**
*(Sussex collection picture)*

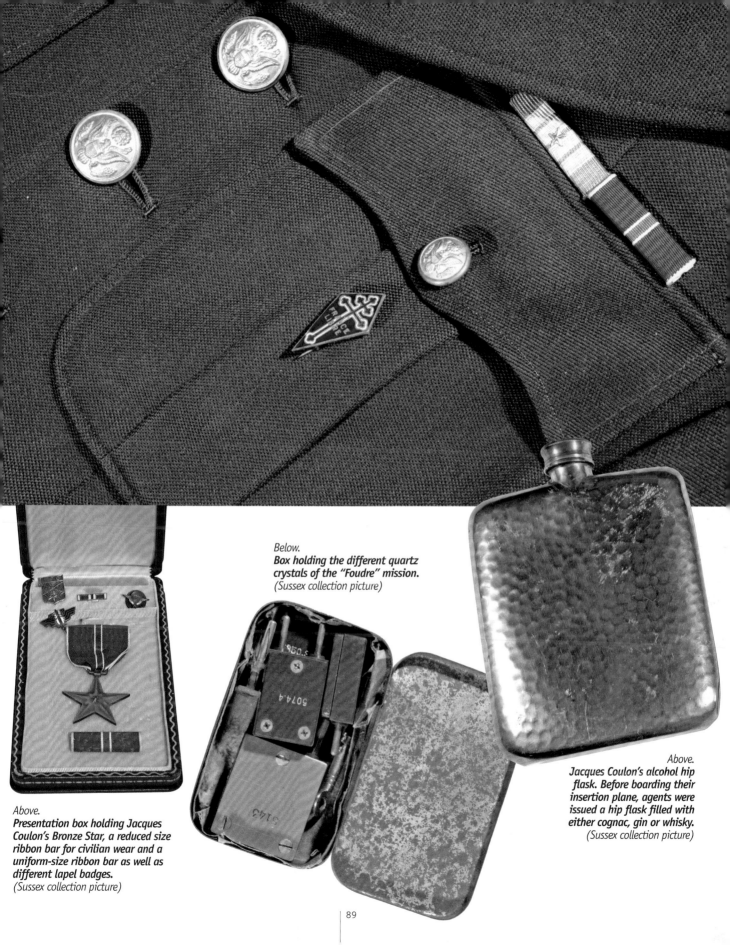

*Below.*
**Box holding the different quartz crystals of the "Foudre" mission.**
*(Sussex collection picture)*

*Above.*
**Presentation box holding Jacques Coulon's Bronze Star, a reduced size ribbon bar for civilian wear and a uniform-size ribbon bar as well as different lapel badges.**
*(Sussex collection picture)*

*Above.*
**Jacques Coulon's alcohol hip flask. Before boarding their insertion plane, agents were issued a hip flask filled with either cognac, gin or whisky.**
*(Sussex collection picture)*

*Opposite.*
**Jacques Coulon's officer quality US Army issue walking out jacket with n°42 Sussex insignia.**
*(Sussex collection picture)*

*Opposite.*
**Jacques Coulon in the city of Amboise in 1945.**
*(Sussex collection picture)*

*Below.*
**A fluorescent ball issued to Jacques Coulon. Each Sussex agent was given such a device, which was designed to help locate equipment in the dark. Some SAS troopers also received this ball.**
*(Sussex collection picture)*

*Below.*
**Jacques Coulon a.k.a "Olivier" OSS identity document.**
*(Sussex collection picture)*

The bearer of this card whose photograph and signature appear hereon, is attached to the United States Armed Forces and is on active duty. Any assistance given him in the performance of his duties will be appreciated. Any inquiries should be directed to the undersigned.

Le porteur de la présente carte, dont la photographie et la signature sont apposées ci-dessus, est attaché à l'Armée des Etats-Unis et est en service actif. Toute assistance qui lui sera donnée dans l'accomplissement de sa mission sera hautement appreciée. Toutes demandes de renseignements complémentaires doivent être addressees au soussigné.

/Lt. OLIVIER, Jacques
*Jolivier*
S/Lt. (Signature of Bearer) Jacques
*William Boyd*
(Official Signature)
1st Lt. William Boyd
Hq., Com. Z (FWD)
Date 12 October 1

# THE "COLÈRE" "SALAUD" AND "FILAN" MISSIONS

Parachuted during the night of 4 July 1944 in Château-l'Hermitage (Sarthe département)

Those three teams were parachuted on 3 July 1944 in the Sarthe département in Château-l'Hermitage. Six agents were inserted: Evelyne Clopet, Roger Fosset, André Noël, Aristide Crocq, Marcel Biscaïno and Laurent Rigot. Their drop was quite eventful, the reception committee having switched the torchlights off too soon. The pilot thought the DZ had been compromised and he brought Evelyne back. She ended up being parachuted on her own four days later but she still managed to link up with her observer on 14 July.

The German were retreating so fast that the initial orders had to be modified accordingly. The agents

*Above.*
**André Rigot a.k.a Laurent the "Filan" mission observer. He was the only agent to survive out of the three teams that were arrested on 9 August 1944 near the city of Vendôme.**
*(Sussex collection picture)*

*Opposite.*
**Hollowed-out signet ring holding a cyanide pill that André Noël a.k.a "Ferrière" had no time to swallow on his arrest. After his execution, the Vendôme gendarmes recovered that ring on André's corpse and gave it to Renée Noël, André's sister.**
*(Photo Christian Viard)*

were now to precede the German retreat without being caught; some résistance fighters provided the agents with a German van and the three teams made their way to Vendôme. On 9 August, fleeing German soldiers hoping to find a lift stopped the van as it was travelling through the village of Lavardin. Taken aback at the sight of those civilians riding inside a German military vehicle, the soldiers immediately asked to see the IDs of the passengers. The agents produced their forged "Ausweis" (German-issued pass) and transportation orders but none of them could speak any German. Maybe the soldiers started wondering whether those civilians had not stolen a German military vehicle or maybe they were just tired and wanted to commandeer this van? They forced the agents to leave the van and threw their belongings on the road; on hitting the road, a suitcase broke open, revealing a radio set; the agents were immediately subjected to a thorough search and weapons were found. They tried to put up a fight but somehow, Evelyne persuaded them not to. The Germans told them to get inside the van; the broke the dividing window and some soldiers sat on the hood while others trained their weapons on the six young agents. Noël and Rigot were sat next to the doors; the van then headed for Vendôme. Biscaïno and Crocq managed to destroy the incriminating documents they were carrying and to throw them out of the vehicle. On reaching Vendôme, Rigot managed to jump from the van and to escape.

*Above.*
*André Noël a.k.a "Ferrière", the "Filan"*
*mission radio operator.*
*(Sussex collection picture)*

*Opposite.*
*Reverse of Sussex insignia n°49 which had been reserved for Marcel Biscaïno a.k.a "Maurin", the "Salaud" mission radio operator. He was executed with four other agents in a quarry located on the Saint-Ouen borough, near Vendôme. This insignia which he was never to receive remained, after the war, in the care of madame Andrée of the Café Sussex in Paris.*
*(Sussex collection picture)*

*Above.*
**Lieutenant Evelyne Clopet a.k.a "Chamonet", the "Colère" mission radio operator. She was executed like her four comrades after having been tortured.**
*(Sussex collection picture)*

*Above.*
**Lieutenant Marcel Biscaïno of the "Salaud" mission.**
*(Sussex collection picture)*

*Opposite.*
**Lieutenant Aristide Crocq a.k.a "Dutal", observer in the "Salaud" mission. Just like his four comrades he was executed after having been tortured.**
*(Sussex collection picture)*

At 2100 hours, the five agents were handed over to the Feldgendarmen. A local cleaning lady reported seeing Evelyne laying on the floor unconscious surrounded by German military policemen. Her forehead showed rifle butt marks and her thighs had been ripped open by lashes. He questioning, punctuated by shouts of pain had lasted until 0130 hours but her tormentors had not managed to get anything of value out of her

The Feldgendarmen had had enough. They had a cart delivered to them and took the five young agents to the Paris roads. The inhabitants of the city of Vendôme heard the squeaking of the cart's axle followed by quick bursts of submachine gun fire. The five martyrs were buried side by side in the small Saint-Ouen cemetery located near Vendôme.

*Opposite.*
**Mementoes of André Noël kept by his sister Renée: signet ring, Sussex insignia n°46, military ID bracelet, posthumous American Silver Star medal and posthumous, post-WW2 pattern French parachute wings n°4560.**
*(Photo Christian Viard)*

*Opposite.*
**Lieutenant Roger Fosset a.k.a "Girard" observer in the "Colère" mission.**
*(Sussex collection picture)*

*Below.*
**Three pages of the post action report (classified as "secret") of the "Filan" mission. André Rigot was the only survivor of that mission.**
*(Document Sussex collection)*

RAPPORT

Equipe: FILAN
Observateur: LAURENT Paul.
FERRIERE André.
Radio

Depart: 3 July
5-7-44 avec les équipes

Arrivée du 2ème avion (équipes
à 1 h 20.

Parachutage par erreur sur le
(signal lettre A - Chef de récept
de CHATEAU-L'HERMITAGE, à 30 km.

COLERE B n'est pas parachuté

Accueil excellent. Les 15
containers de matériel destiné
sont placés en forêt dans une
d'armes attendus.

Les quatre équipes sont c
5, la Maison radio est tentée

Le 5 au soir, les équipes
familles du village.

Liaison radio essayée à
nous demandons l'envoi d'un

La liaison est diffici
que FERRIERE réussit à 1/8
ce qui est de la liaison r

Par broadcast nous so
prévenu, et nous l'attend

Entre temps, COLERE

Le 17, les quatre é
abandonée, au milieu de

Au bout de plusieu
observateurs décident
été données. Nous

GERARD (équipe CO
qui devait le reseau
dev

... Roger P
... de son frère à DREUX. M
... très bien, m'héberge pendant deux jou
s'offre à me procurer les asiles nécessaires, de
mateurs, des accus, etc...

Je rentre à CHATEAU L'HERMITAGE le 7/8 au soir.

L'éclaireur RAYMONDE est venue pendant mon absen
a indiqué un moyen de transport vers PARIS, par auto
postale.

Le 8, FERRIERE va AU MANS dans l'intention d'achete
une remorque pour velo, destinée au transport de notre
matériel. Avant LE MANS un barrage allemand lui fait
faire demi tour.

A son retour, il trouve les troupes américains sur la
route du MANS: nous ne pouvons donc plus monter directemen
sur DREUX.

Par broadcast, nous recevons des adresses à PARIS,
les équipes COLERE et SALAUD décident de s'y rendre.

Nous sommes prêts à partir le 9/8; et
faire un large détour par l'est
où, en ce qui concerne

Un

*Above.*
**On 23 April 1945, Brigadier General B. Rogers (ETO) presents madame Amélie Noël the Silver Star medal posthumously awarded to her son André.**
*(Sussex collection picture)*

*Opposite.*
**The monument to the memory of the five agents executed by the Germans has been moved several times in the recent past. It is now located on the Saint Ouen borough in the locality of La Croix-Montjoie.**
*(Sussex collection)*

# THE "DENTELLES" MISSION

Parachuted on 7 July 1944 in Fouilleuse (Oise département)

Area of operation: Alençon (Orne département)
End of mission: 13 August 1944
Lieutenant Christian de Sorbier a.k.a "Louis Blanc" (observer)
Lieutenant Pierre Ravarre a.k.a "Jean Vernez" (radio operator)

THIS MISSION was cut short because of the speed of the American forces' advance. Those two agents were parachuted a second time in September 1944 *"see the "Montre" Mission, page 122".*

*Opposite.*
*Lieutenant Pierre Ravarre a.k.a Vernez the "Dentelle" mission radio operator.*
*(Sussex collection picture)*

*Below.*
*BCRA ID card in the name of "Vernez" belonging to Pierre Ravarre.*
*(Sussex collection picture)*

*Opposite.*
*Pierre Ravarre a.k.a "Vernez" CFLN card.*
*(Sussex collection picture)*

COMITE FRANÇAIS de la Liberation Nationale

B. R. A. L.

GRADE *maréchal des logis*
NOM VERNEZ
PRENOMS Jean

Signature du Titulaire :

*Vernez*

No. 1306

CARTE D'IDENTITÉ

SOUS-OFFICIER ou Homme de Troupe

M. VERNEZ
Prénoms : Jean
Surnom :
Grade : *Maréchal des Logis*
Date de nomination : 20-12-42
Arme : *Artillerie*
Unité 67e R A A
Classe 1942
Nationalité : *Française*
Nationalité à la naissance : *Française*
Lieu de naissance : *Mourmelon le Grand*
Pays : *France* Département : *Marne*
Date de naissance : 20/12/1922
Autorité militaire ayant délivré la carte : BCRA
No de la carte : 30258
A *Alger*, le 11/12 1943

*Opposite.*
**Lieutenant Christian de Sorbier a.k.a "Louis Blanc", observer in the "Dentelles" mission.**
*(Sussex collection picture)*

*Opposite.*
**Reverse of Pierre Ravarre's a.k.a "Vernez" CFLN card.**
*(Sussex collection picture)*

*Opposite.*
**Pierre Ravarre's hip flask.**
*(Sussex collection picture)*

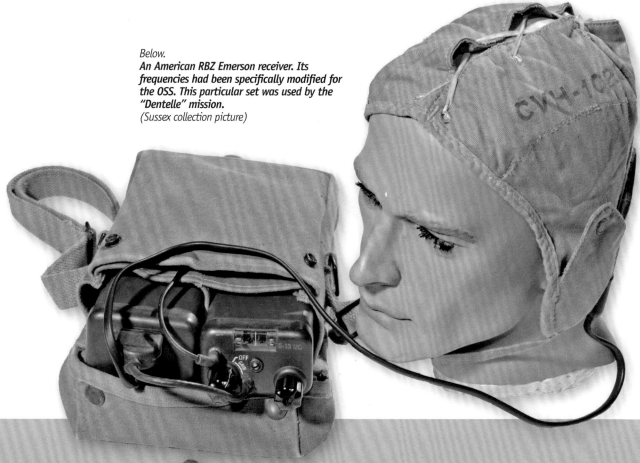

*Below.*
**An American RBZ Emerson receiver. Its frequencies had been specifically modified for the OSS. This particular set was used by the "Dentelle" mission.**
*(Sussex collection picture)*

*Opposite.*
**This very sturdy cardboard suitcase held radio equipment and miscelaneous kit. It was fitted inside a "Dentelle" mission container; notice the "111B" marking daubed with white paint on the side of the suitcase.**
*(Sussex collection picture)*

*Opposite.*
**Close up view on the lock, which bears British markings.**
*(Sussex collection picture)*

*Opposite.*
**The hinges of the suitcase are also marked with different informations that leave little doubt on its origin...**
*(Sussex collection picture)*

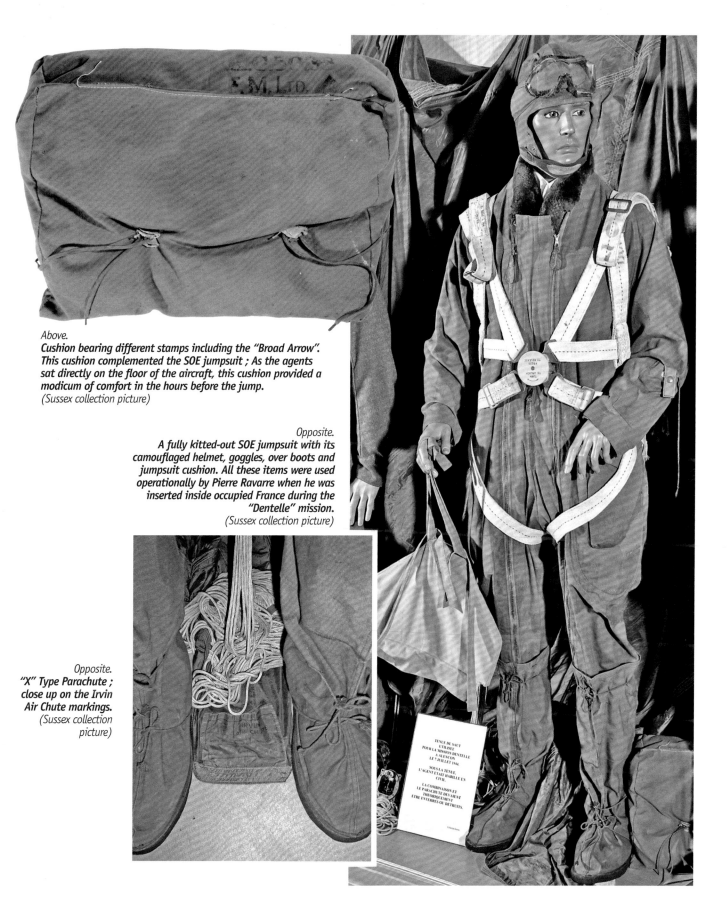

*Above.*
**Cushion bearing different stamps including the "Broad Arrow".**
**This cushion complemented the SOE jumpsuit ; As the agents**
**sat directly on the floor of the aircraft, this cushion provided a**
**modicum of comfort in the hours before the jump.**
*(Sussex collection picture)*

*Opposite.*
**A fully kitted-out SOE jumpsuit with its**
**camouflaged helmet, goggles, over boots and**
**jumpsuit cushion. All these items were used**
**operationally by Pierre Ravarre when he was**
**inserted inside occupied France during the**
**"Dentelle" mission.**
*(Sussex collection picture)*

*Opposite.*
**"X" Type Parachute ;**
**close up on the Irvin**
**Air Chute markings.**
*(Sussex collection*
*picture)*

# THE "HÉLÈNE" MISSION

BCRA, OSSEX

Area of operation: Troyes (Aube département)
Lieutenant Albert Beaurel a.k.a "Pierre Dubost" (observer)
Lieutenant Louis Guyomard a.k.a "Pierre Deniel" (radio operator)

*Opposite.*
**Lieutenant Louis Guyomard a.k.a "Pierre Deniel",
the "Hélène" mission radio operator.**
*(Sussex collection)*

*Above.*
**Louis
Guyomard's bullion
Free French parachute
wings on blue backing.**
*(Sussex collection)*

*Below.*
**Reverse of Louis Guyomard's forged identity
card in the name of Le Flohic.**
*(Sussex collection)*

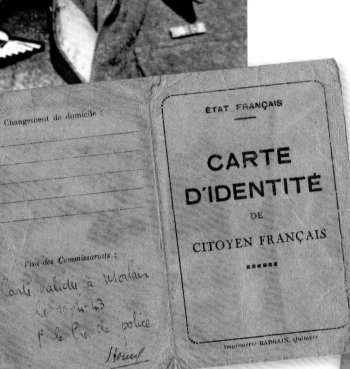

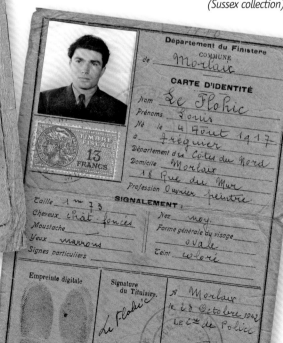

*Opposite.*
**The forged identity card Louis Guyomard used
during his mission.**
*(Sussex collection)*

This team was parachuted on 8 July 1944 in Orbais-l'Abbaye (Marne département)

Some incidents took place during this mission, as reported by Louis Guyomard, the team's radio operator:

On 21 August 1944, Guyomard was on his bike riding toward Verrière, the location he had selected to hide his emergency radio set when he was caught between two Feldgendarmen checkpoints at the entrance of the village of Pont-Sainte-Marie, 4 km away from his safe house. His only way out was to try and go across the woods that were bordering the road with all his equipment. The Germans, 50 metres away, saw him and opened fire; abandoning both his bicycle and his radio set, Guyomart managed to returned safely home. Two days later, he returned to the scene only to find that his bicycle and radio equipment had disappeared!

During its deployment, this team sent very good intelligence reports, particularly on the fuel dumps located in Brevennes, which was eventually bombed and completely destroyed. It also reported the road movements of German troops as well as the arrival by train of Wehrmacht reinforcements coming from Belgium; also, it identified the "Leibstandarte Adolf Hitler" SS Division near the city of Troyes.

The mission was finally completed on 15 September 1944. Albert Beaurel and Louis Guyomard both received the Silver Star from the American high command in recognition of the heroic deeds they performed during "Hélène".

*Opposite.*
**A very rare FFI codebook printed on material. This particular book was used by Lieutenant Ronin, one of the commanders of the D'Orbais-L'Abbaye maquis, who gave it to Louis Guyomard at the end of his mission.**
*(Sussex collection picture)*

*Opposite.*
**Louis Guyomard's well-worn Denison smock. He used this smock in training, during the Germany campaign and finally in Indochina when Guyomard was part of the Commando Conus.**
*(Sussex collection)*

Opposite.
The file and escape compass were two of the most commonly found items in Sussex agents escape and evasion kit. These two items belonged to Louis Guyomard. The shape of the file was such that it could be hidden inside the fly of a trouser.
(Sussex collection picture)

Opposite.
A forged work certificate used by Louis Guyomard.
(Sussex collection picture)

Below.
Reverse of the forged work certificate supposedly delivered by the "Maison Guillou" a paint and glass business located in the city of Morlaix.
(Sussex collection picture).

Opposite.
Louis Guyomard's Type X parachute quick release buckle.
(Sussex collection picture)

*Opposite.*
**Louis Guyomard resting somewhere in the United Kingdom between two missions. He wears a Battle Dress and a black beret with a Parachute Regiment badge minus its crown. The Sussex insignia and the Free French para wings are much in evidence.**
*(Sussex collection picture)*

*Opposite.*
**"Emergency frequency" crystal quartz of the "Hélène" mission.**
*(Sussex collection picture)*

*Opposite.*
**Tactical aide memoire (blown up for clarity) used by Louis Guyomard on operation.**
*(Sussex collection picture)*

*Opposite.*
**Demobilization certificate in the name of Le Flohic. This forged document is one of the many official papers each Sussex agent carried with him at all time.**
*(Sussex collection picture)*

# THE "BEAUHARNAIS" MISSION

BRISSEX

BCRA

## Parachuted on 20 July 1944 in Souppes-sur-Loing (Seine-et-Marne département)

Area of operation: city of Saint-Germain
End of mission: on liberation of Saint-Germain at the end of the month of August 1944
Lieutenant Porlier a.k.a "Carlier" (observer)
Lieutenant Emile Gendarme a.k.a "Desmarchais" (radio operator)

*Opposite.*
**Lieutenant Emile Gendarme, radio operator for the "Beauharnais" mission.**
*(Sussex collection picture)*

*Below.*
**A .38 caliber "Faultless" tear gas throwing pistol in its original delivery box with two rounds. All Sussex agents were issued such a device.**
*(Sussex collection)*

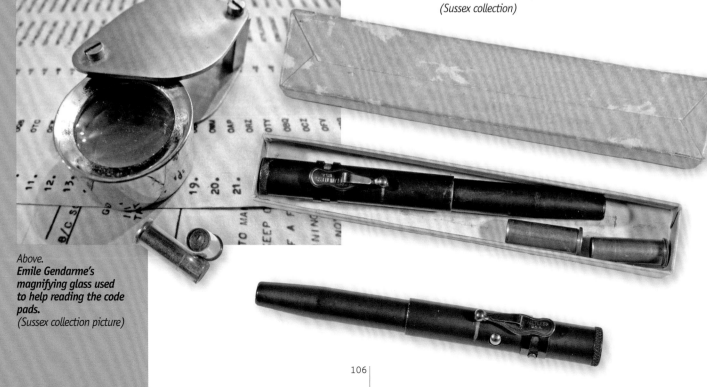

*Above.*
**Emile Gendarme's magnifying glass used to help reading the code pads.**
*(Sussex collection picture)*

*Opposite.*
**Lieutenant Raymond Porlier a.k.a "Carlier", the observer of the "Beauharnais" mission.**
*(Sussex collection picture)*

*Opposite.*
**Loading a round into the "Faultless".**
*(Sussex collection picture)*

FAULTLESS
U.S.A.

*Opposite.*
**Close up on the marking of the .38 caliber tear gas throwing pistol located on the pocket clip.**
*(Sussex collection picture)*

# The "Daru" Mission

*Opposite.*
**Lieutenant Raymond Mocquet a.k.a "Vermuge",
observer of the "Daru" mission.**
*(Sussex collection picture)*

1944

---

**Parachuted on 4 August 1944
in Orbais-L'Abbaye**

Area of operation: city of Sézanne
End of mission: 1st of September 1944
Lieutenant Raymond Mocquet a.k.a "Daniel Dumont" (observer)
Lieutenant Lucien Bignon a.k.a "Rogier" (radio operator)
(Extract from the unpublished memories of Raymond Mocquet,
with the author's kind autorisation)

## MISSION IN FRANCE – 4 AUGUST 1944

ON FRIDAY 23 JUNE, *I linked up with the Sussex plan
organisation in Praewood House in Saint Alban.
There was a lot of classwork and I spent hours on
German weapons recognition and on the use of cyphers.
With the Sussex plan organisation, the officers were
really splendid chaps, especially Colonel Henderson,
Captain Wingate and American Lieutenant Kennedy.
Finally, we were transferred to Orwell Grange, near
Cambridge in order to prepare for our parachute
insertion into France.
We drew our kit and received two pairs of shoes, two
second-hand suits so as not to be too conspicuous while
in France, a Colt pistol, a combat knife, a knuckle duster,
a compass, a ring with a hidden compass which only
showed North, a brush with a hidden compartment
used to hide messages, a flask of brandy and a hundred
packets of Gauloises cigarettes that would prove most
useful to thank all my volunteer informers. I thus
decided to quit smoking. I also did not forget my cyanide
pill, which I hid in a fold near to my trouser belt.
We also were given some new codes, the maps of our
future area of operations, which was centred on the city
of Givet in the Ardennes. I was given a new identity card
as well as the cover story that went with it. I was now
called "Dumont Daniel" born on 18 November 1926
which meant I was now three years younger than my
real age. I was supposed to live on 39, Rue de Lille, in
Paris and to work in the city of Argenteuil in a company
specialising in mechanical work and aircraft parts. I had*

to keep me at all time an employment certificate (signed by the management of the company which employed me) as well as some ration cards.

Lucien was also given his new ID papers as well as his radio sets. During the week prior to our parachute insertion, we familiarised ourselves with our new identities. In a public garden, a British officer suddenly called out my real name: "Vermuge !". It took me one tenth of a second to forget I no longer was called Vermuge but "Dumont". That same officer asked me how I normally commuted from my flat in Paris to my work in Argenteuil, which train I took, which metro station I used or where I normally bought my bread when in Paris. The truth was that during that period, you had to register yourself with a specific baker if you wanted to buy bread. I did not have answers to all those questions. The officer gave me a map of the metro to locate the nearest station to my supposed flat, a phone directory to find a bakery, etc. They were dead serious and left nothing to chance. On the financial side, we were given 200,000 francs for each team, which was a huge sum for that period.

We were scheduled to jump during the night of the 2nd to the 3rd of August. The coded sentence which was supposed to be broadcasted from London to the reception committee was "Mexico a plein pouvoir". We waited. Nothing was heard on the 2nd of August. Our departure had been postponed because of bad weather. Finally, on the evening of the 3rd of August, we heard the message "Mexico a plein pouvoir"; we were overwhelmed with joy but quickly started our final preparations before driving to the airfield. We boarded the aircraft on the 3rd of August at 2300 hours. Soon after midnight, a crewmember informed us we were nearing the French coasts. We received a "salute" from the German flak and finally, we reached our DZ.

There were eight of us and we were dropped in two sticks of four. Since we jumped through a hole in the floor and that only four paratroopers could seat at any one time around this hatch, there was no other choice. The first stick probably jumped at a height of roughly 200 metres while the second jumped a little closer to the ground, probably no more than a hundred and fifty metres. In order to remain hidden from view, the plane did some contour flying. When time came for the second stick to jump, the red light turned to green and the British dispatcher shouted "Go!".

I landed in the worst possible way, my back being the first part of my body to hit the ground. Lulu, who had landed just before me confirmed that my parachute was not fully inflated and had taken the shape of a pear before I had hit the ground. I was unable to stand up! Someone unbuckled my harness; I was in a lot of pain. I

was put in a butcher's van and taken to a schoolmistress who lived with her brother.

While the other seven agents were congratulating each other on a successful jump, I was put to bed and given painkillers. The next morning, a doctor belonging to the résistance visited me. Ideally, I should have gotten an X-ray to see what was wrong with me but at the moment it was just impossible as the Gestapo was checking all the hospitals in the region; the plane, which had dropped us, had been heard and the Germans were

Opposite.
**Lieutenant Lucien Bignon a.k.a "Rogier".**
(Sussex collection picture)

*Above.*
**The suitcase used to carry the Mark 7 radio set, its power pack, accessories, headset, crystal quartz, etc.**
*(Sussex collection picture)*

*Opposite.*
**The same brush in the closed position. Raymond Mocquet used this particular brush on operation.**
*(Sussex collection picture)*

*Opposite.*
**Cloth brush with a hidden compartment used to store messages or small items.**
*(Sussex collection picture)*

looking for agents who could have gotten injured during their jump. We were supposed to operate in Givet so we first headed for Rheims. A priest welcomed us and provided us with some forged ID documents. Lulu became a religious school inspector and I was supposed to have just received a new posting as a trainee teacher in Givet. On that night, I slept with some local folks who had given me their daughter's bedroom for the occasion. The fighters always get a mention in war stories but never those anonymous helpers who were risking their lives and their families to hide us. Lucien stayed with another family.

On the next day, we had to ride on bicycles to our

*destination while our equipment was supposed to reach Givet in the lorry of a coal merchant. We were just about to leave the priest's house when the coal merchant arrived and told us "Do not leave now, I do not want to carry your equipment. The family who was going to house us in Givet has been arrested. I don't know if they have spoken under torture but all the lorries are systematically emptied as they enter Givet."*

*Lucien recovered his radio set and set up shop in the presbytery. He sent the message I had encoded. London learnt of those arrests at the same time as we did and the top brass feared we might fall into a trap. We got the order to leave for the city of Sézanne where we had some contacts. We were told to establish an intelligence-gathering network. I was housed with a family of résistants. Lucien found lodging in Plessis, a hamlet located a few kilometres from were I was. My bedroom overlooked a crossroad, which was in fact more like a plaza, on which there was a constant movement of German troops. That was an outstanding observation post. I also had an unlikely informer in the person of Guy Picot, aged 13 or 14. He knew his older brother was part of the résistance and that he took part in sabotage operations but this older brother did not take into consideration the thirst for action of his younger sibling. Guy wanted to prove he also could take part to résistance*

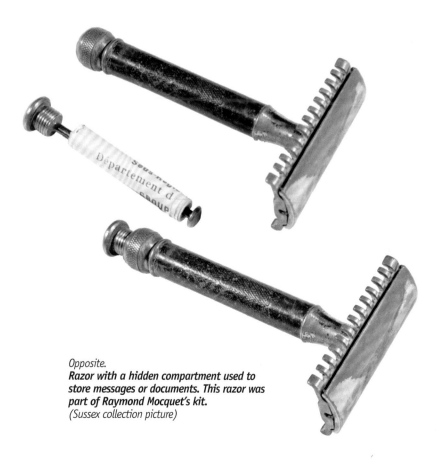

*activities; he offered to get close to the Germans because it was easy to do so considering his young age. He thus jumped on his bike with a basket full of tomatoes and fruits; he told the Germans he had stolen them in the garden of his father and that he wanted to exchange the fruits and vegetables against some cigarettes. In this way, he got into a clearing where tanks and other vehicles were parked. I had told him how to identify them thanks to their main armament; for example, the muzzle brake at the end of the barrel of the Tiger tank looked a bit like a honeycomb. On the day of the liberation, I offered him my commando dagger as well as an FFI armband. His older brother was extremely surprised that "junior" had never mentioned him our relationship. On my recommendation, Guy was to receive a certificate from the Allies praising his courage.*

*One day, Lucien told me that he thought he had been DF'd by the Germans. I decided to bring him back to Sézanne and took my bicycle, along with a trailer, to pick him up. We put all his equipment in the trailer and then covered it with some beetroot leaves. We then arrived on the square in the middle of the hamlet, opposite a German truck and about twenty soldiers who were getting into formation, waiting for some orders. Meanwhile, we cycled past them. Five or six minutes latter, they started searching the five or six houses composing the hamlet, including the one that had been sheltering Lucien.*

*Liberation arrived on 28 August. There were many casualties in Sézanne. First of all, Robert Jouarre was shot while going over a wall trying to escape a German checkpoint. Eleven other résistants were killed in action in Gaye after a contact with over fifty well-armed SS troops. Nevertheless, some operations were highly successful. Some FFIs, under the orders of Gustave Jouarre had located a German troop-carrying train, which had stopped alongside a platform just after the Sézanne station. They reported its location. I coded*

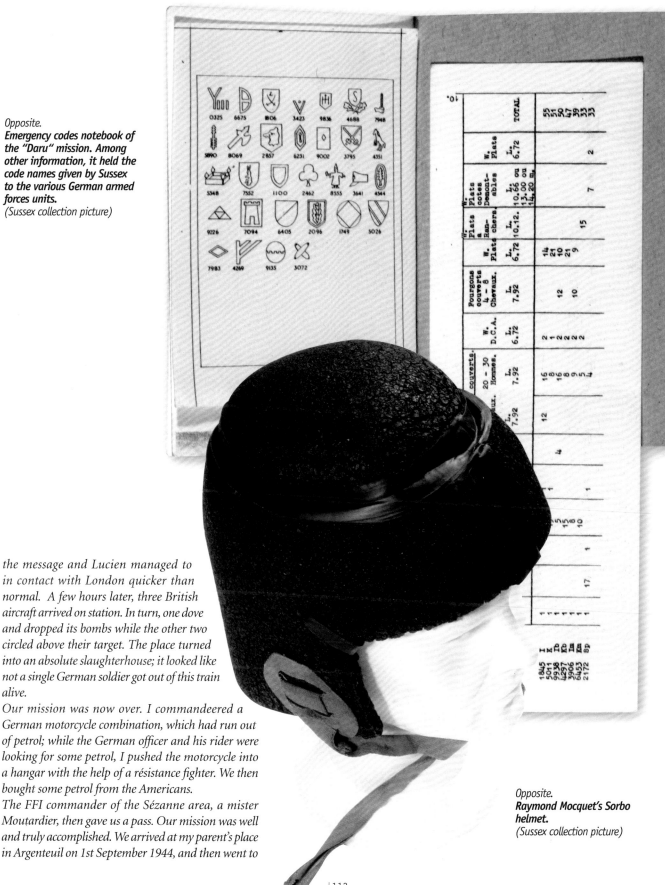

Opposite.
**Emergency codes notebook of the "Daru" mission.** Among other information, it held the code names given by Sussex to the various German armed forces units.
(Sussex collection picture)

the message and Lucien managed to in contact with London quicker than normal. A few hours later, three British aircraft arrived on station. In turn, one dove and dropped its bombs while the other two circled above their target. The place turned into an absolute slaughterhouse; it looked like not a single German soldier got out of this train alive.

Our mission was now over. I commandeered a German motorcycle combination, which had run out of petrol; while the German officer and his rider were looking for some petrol, I pushed the motorcycle into a hangar with the help of a résistance fighter. We then bought some petrol from the Americans.

The FFI commander of the Sézanne area, a mister Moutardier, then gave us a pass. Our mission was well and truly accomplished. We arrived at my parent's place in Argenteuil on 1st September 1944, and then went to

Opposite.
**Raymond Mocquet's Sorbo helmet.**
(Sussex collection picture)

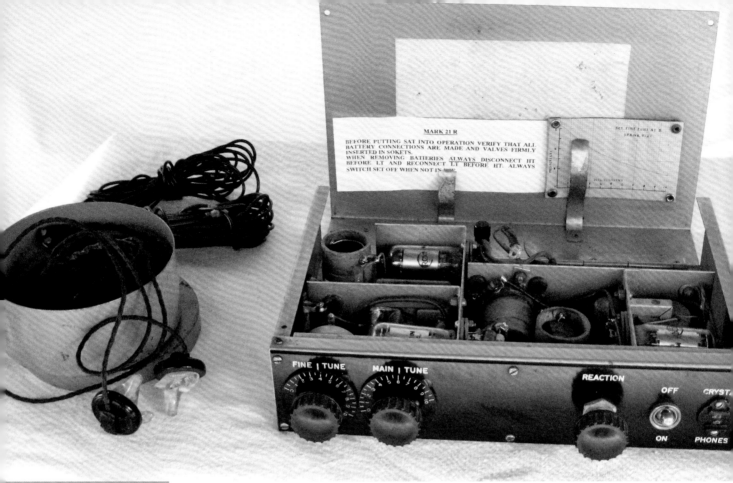

MARK 21 R

BEFORE PUTTING SAT INTO OPERATION VERIFY THAT ALL
BATTERY CONNECTIONS ARE MADE AND VALVES FIRMLY
INSERTED IN SOKETS.
WHEN REMOVING BATTERIES ALWAYS DISCONNECT HT
BEFORE LT AND RECONNECT LT BEFORE HT. ALWAYS
SWITCH SET OFF WHEN NOT IN USE.

*Above.*
**Mark XXI emergency transceiver used
by Pierre Ravarre. The miniature
headsets are of the Piezo type.**
*(Georges Ducreuzet picture collection)*

*Opposite.*
**Close up view of the Mark XXI
transceiver and of the small Biley
quartz.**
*(Georges Ducreuzet picture collection)*

# The "Montre" Mission

Parachuted on 2 September 1944 in the Granges Maillots (45 km South East of the city of Besançon, in the Doubs département)

Area of operation: cities of Besançon and Valdahon
End of mission: 25 October 1944
Lieutenant Christian de Sorbier a.k.a "Louis Blanc" (observer)
Lieutenant Pierre Ravarre a.k.a "Jean Vernez" (radio)

*Above.*
**US M1 Carbine used by Pierre Ravarre during his second mission in the Vosges département in September 1944.**
*(Sussex collection picture)*

*Opposite.*
**The classic Type "C" container. There were two such containers for each "Sussex" agent.**
*(Sussex collection picture)*

*Below.*
**SSTR-1 emergency transceiver.**
*(Sussex collection picture)*

*Opposite.*
**Lieutenant Roland Sadoun a.k.a "Sauvagnac" in the St-Alban gardens in Great-Britain.**
*(Sussex collection picture)*

*Opposite.*
**The .38 calibre Webley revolver Roland Sadoun used during the combat operations that led to the liberation of Paris.**

BCRA, OSSEX

BRISSEX

# "T-FORCE" SUSSEX
## TEAMS IN THE LIBERATION OF PARIS

*Opposite.*
**German "war trophies" seized by Roland Sadoun during the liberation of Paris : an SS dagger and a small flag.**
*(Sussex collection picture)*

*Opposite.*
***Lieutenant René Razaire a.k.a "Rigal" took part in different "Sussex" intelligence gathering missions in Paris.***
*(Sussex collection picture)*

U<small>NDER THE COMMAND OF</small> C<small>OLONEL</small> T<small>OMPKINS</small>, some teams were given priority when it came to entering the capital of France. This particular aspect of the Sussex mission is not very well known. It saw the integration of some Sussex teams with the "T-Force", a special unit which operated directly in support of the staff of General Bradley's 12th Army Group. Even though the "T-Force" was essentially composed of American servicemen, some BCRA members, such as "Colonel Rémy" were also part of it.

Roland Sadoun a.k.a "Sauvagnac", René Razaire a.k.a "Rigal", who both had been injured in training while in Saint Albans, but also Lieutenant Michel Tillet a.k.a "Marcel Treville" who all had missed out on the parachute insertions of the Summer took part in those intelligence gathering missions, first in Normandy and then in Paris with Guy Wingate. They landed in Normandy in July 1944 and started by conducting some interrogations of German POWs in the area. They used a farm in the vicinity of Formigny as their HQ. Then, the team headed for Paris with General Leclerc's Free French 2nd Armoured Division. During that period which was marked first by a popular insurgency and then by the liberation of the capital city of France, the Sussex agents operated both inside and outside Paris. Their main task was to locate the archives of the Abwehr and to obtain a list of the agents that would likely turn against their former employer. Guy Wingate found a treasure throve of information in the famous hotel Majestic, the former location of the German headquarters in Paris. During the combat operations conducted in the East of France in the Ardennes, in Lorraine, in Alsace and in the Colmar pocket and eventually in Germany, other infiltration and intelligence gathering missions were conducted by a number of Sussex teams. Each of the Sussex agents took an active part in the intelligence collection effort organised to provide the Allied supreme command with a clear picture of the situation. On more than one occasion, the agents followed the German by hiding in the midst of the retreating units. When hostilities ended in Europe, some of them transferred to the Pacific theatre of operations and took part in combat operations against the Japanese as part of the "Commando Conus" or of "Force 136". But this is another story…

*Bullion parachute wings. That type of wings was often seen on Sussex agents belonging to the "Brissex" part of the plan. Initially, that set of wings was sewn on Roland Sadoun's Battle Dress.*
*(Sussex collection picture)*

*Below.*
*René Razaire's British steel helmet with camouflage net cover camouflage. This particular helmet was worn both while in the United Kingdom and during the liberation of Paris.*
*(Sussex collection picture)*

*Below.*
***OSS escape knife which belonged René Razaire. This tool had a plier, several files, a tire burster and a straight blade.***
*(Sussex collection picture)*

*Opposite.*
**Lieutenant Michel Tillet a.k.a "Treville" who also took part in different "Sussex" intelligence gathering missions in Paris but with the Free French 2nd Armoured Division.**
*(Sussex collection picture)*

*Below.*
**Michel Tillet's Free French wings in silver.**
*(Sussex collection picture)*

GOUVERNEMENT PROVISOIRE
DE LA
REPUBLIQUE FRANCAISE

Paris le 19 Octobre 1944

RESEAU SUSSEX

ATTESTATION

Je soussigné, Lieutenant Colonel Lefebvre, Chef des réseaux Sussex et Proust certifie que Monsieur Tréville est un agent Sussex.

Lieutenant Colonel Lefebvre
Chef des Réseaux Sussex et Proust
Bureau 315
N.B. Cet agent est assimilé au grad de Sous-Lieutenant

*Above.*
**Michel Tillet's Sussex and Proust certificates.**
*(Sussex collection picture)*

*Opposite.*
**OSS Collapsible baton used by Roland Sadoun.**
*(Sussex collection picture)*

*Opposite.*
**Battle Dress Pattern 40 of Roland Sadoun.**
*(Sussex collection picture)*

*Below.*
**Close up on Roland Sadoun's Lieutenant slides, gold metal "France" title and bullion parachute wings.**
*(Sussex collection picture)*

*Opposite.*
**OSS-issued Colt 1911 shoulder holster used by Roland Sadoun.**
*(Sussex collection picture)*

Issued to **Capt** **Guy Wingate**
Rank        Name        ASN

Pass No **482**

Identity Document No **A 500237**

Authority to enter buildings or areas guarded by ''T'' FORCE, in **Paris** and to examine and remove documents and equipment with the understanding that anything removed is turned into ''T'' FORCE HEADQUARTERS.

Issued by ... Lt. Col.

*Above.*
**T-Force pass in the name of Captain Guy Wingate.**
*(Sussex collection picture)*

*Opposite.*
**21 Army Group cloth patch. The T-Force was attached to this Army Group and this patch was kept by Roland Sadoun as a memento.**
*(Sussex collection picture)*

*Below.*
**Very seldom seen OSS .22 long rifle Stinger pen guns. They were stored in packets of ten. These Stingers belonged to Roland Sadoun.**
*(Sussex collection picture)*

*Opposite.*
**A watercolour painted in July 1944 by Captain Guy Wingate. The farm visible on this work is located in Formigny in the Calvados departement. For a few days, it was used as the HQ of the "Sussex Normandie" team.**
*(Sussex collection picture)*

# Various artifacts recovered by Roland Sadoun during the liberation of Paris

The neck ribbon of a Knight's Cross of the Iron Cross.

Nazi flag seized during the liberation of Paris.

German Cross in Gold.

German ribbon bar.

Early version of an SS dagger.

The neck ribbon of a Knight's Cross of the Iron Cross.

# Other losses SUSSEX : The "Murat" mission

1943

*Opposite.*
**Lieutenant Georges Emile Muller a.k.a "Gaston Marchand".**
*(Sussex collection)*

*Opposite.*
**Lieutenant Guy Mignonneau a.k.a "Martin", observer of the "Marmont" mission.**
*(Sussex collection picture)*

Lieutenant Georges Emile Muller a.k.a "Gaston Marchand", assigned to the "Murat" mission, was parachuted on 6 July 1944 with Refanche a.k.a "Thenet", his radio operator, in order to carry out an intelligence gathering mission near the cities of Soissons and Compiègne. According to his grandson, Navy Lieutenant Junet-Muller, *Lieutenant Muller and Devilers as well as an American known as "Kalif" were killed in action while fighting elements of a Panzer Division located in the bois de Châssis near the village of Vic-sur-Aisne between Soissons and Compiègne. According to some local sources, they had been betrayed and then given some false information that had led them directly into a German ambush.*

# THE "SOULT" MISSION

THAT TEAM WAS MADE UP OF GUY MIGNONNEAU a.k.a "Martin" as observer and Delplanque a.k.a "Cornu" as radio operator. It was parachuted on 20 July 1944 in the vicinity of the town of Suippes. From there, they reached the city of Lille where they were supposed to start their mission. There are very few details available on the circumstances of his arrest, but it appears that Guy Mignonneau, like many other Sussex agents, was betrayed. On 7 August Guy Mignonneau, who had a number of urgent messages to transmit to London went to the Institut Diderot in Lille, one of the broadcasting locations favoured by his team. Unfortunately, the Gestapo soon surrounded the building. Guy Mignonneau was quickly arrested and locked under guard in a classroom. Nevertheless, he managed to escape his guard's attention and to overpower him. He then jumped out of a window and into the street. The alarm was given and Guy Mignonneau was hit in the back by a burst fired by a German submachine gun. Grievously wounded, he was taken to hospital but died the same evening. Nobody ever knew what became of his teammate Delplanque.

## SUSSEX AGENTS KILLED IN ACTION

| Name | Alias | Role | OSSEX/ BRISSEX | Mission name | Insertion Date | Remarks |
|---|---|---|---|---|---|---|
| BINET Pierre | GAUDIN / LUCIEN | Radio Operator | Brissex | Pathfinder I | 08/02/44 | Shot by firing squad on 19 August 1944 |
| VOYER Jacques | VOYER | Observer | Ossex | Vitrail | 10/04/44 | Arrested on 10 June. Shot by firing squad on 27 June 1944 |
| ANCERGUES | ASNIER | Radio Operator | Brissex | Pathfinder II | 09/05/44 | Shot by firing squad on 19 August 1944 |
| GUYOMAR Claude | GOUDELIN | Observer | Brissex | Ney | 10/05/44 | Shot by firing squad on 3 August 1944 |
| MILLET Lucien | MARCHAND | Radio Operator | Brissex | Ney | 10/05/44 | Shot by firing squad on 31 August 1944 |
| ROUPAIN Bernard | FRANCOIS | Observer | Brissex | Foy | 28/05/44 | Arrested on 5 August. Deported, never to return to France. |
| GIRBAL Jacques | FOURNIERE | Radio Operator | Brissex | Foy | 28/05/44 | Arrested on 5 August. Deported, never to return to France |
| BISCAÏNO Marcel | MAURIN | Radio Operator | Ossex | Salaud | 03/07/44 | Arrested on 9 August. Shot by firing squad on 10 August 1944 |
| CROCQ Aristide | DUTAL | Observer | Ossex | Salaud | 03/07/44 | Arrested on 9 August. Shot by firing squad on 10 August 1944 |
| FOSSET Roger | GIRARD | Observer | Ossex | Colère | 03/07/44 | Arrested on 9 August. Shot by firing squad on 10 August 1944 |
| NOËL André | FERRIERE | Radio Operator | Ossex | Filan | 03/07/44 | Arrested on 9 August. Shot by firing squad on 10 August 1944 |
| MULLER Emile | MARCHAND | Observer | Brissex | Murat | 05/07/44 | Shot by firing squad on 31 August 1944 |
| CLOPET Evelyne | CHAMONET | Radio Operator | Ossex | Colère | 08/07/44 | Arrested on 9 August. Shot by firing squad on 10 August 1944 |
| MIGNONNEAU Louis | MARTIN | Observateur | Brissex | Soult | 20/07/44 | Arrested on 5 August. Deported, never to return to France. |

## DEPORTED SUSSEX AGENTS SUSSEX WHO ARE KNOWN TO HAVE RETURNED FROM CAPTIVITY

| Name | Alias | Role | OSSEX BRISSEX | Mission name | Insertion Date | Remarks |
|---|---|---|---|---|---|---|
| LASSALE Georges | LESCOUR | Observer | Ossex | Pathfinder I | 08/02/44 | Deported- survived |
| CLÉMENT Georges | CLAUZEL | Observer | Ossex | Plainchant | 09/04/44 | Deported- survived |
| LACQUEMANT | PICOT | Observer | Brissex | Junot | 28/05/44 | Deported- survived |
| BECK René | CAUMONT | Radio Operator | Brissex | Junot | 28/05/44 | Deported- survived |

| | | | | | | |
|---|---|---|---|---|---|---|
| 14 | agents P2 | Parachuted and killed in operation or in captivity | | 4 | agents P2 | Parachuted, deported and returned |
| 13 | agents P2 | Recruited in France and killed, including four in captivity | | 6 | agents P2 | Recruited in France deported and returned |

# THE "SUSSEX" BADGE

BCRA, OSSEX BRISSEX

*Below.*
**Lapel-size Sussex insignia. Only a very limited number of this item was produced (2 finishes were available). The full-size insignia also existed with different finishes : a limited run with serial number comprized between 1 à 101 and a needle on the reverse and another run of about thirty, without a serial number and with rings on the reverse.**
*(Sussex collection picture)*

*Opposite.*
**Lapel-size Sussex insignia. Only a very limited number of this item was produced (2 finishes were available). The full-size insignia also existed with different finishes : a limited run with serial number comprized between 1 à 101 and a needle on the reverse and another run of about thirty, without a serial number and with rings on the reverse.**
*(Sussex collection picture)*

125

# A café named Sussex

*Opposite.*
**The Café Sussex after the war ; it had received a new coat of paint courtesy of some British MI6 agents.**
*(Sussex collection picture)*

**Plus de cent parachutistes**
sont passés PENDANT LES QUATRE ANS D'OCCUPATION
dans ce petit café parisien

« J'AI EU CINQ FUSILLÉS, NOUS DIT CELLE
QUI FUT LEUR MÈRE, ET UN TORTURE »

In 1928, a young couple became the owner of a small café situated on rue Tournefort, in Paris' fifth arrondissement. This couple, Raymond and Andrée Goubillon, led a peaceful life until the Second World War began. In September 1939, Raymond joined the armed forces. He was taken as a POW and sent to Stalag 9-C in Erfurt from which he only returned in May 1945. Andrée remained on her own in Paris and did the best she could to run her small business. Contacted by "Jeannette" who looked for safe houses for Sussex plan agents, Andrée Goubillon was soon to turn into a major facilitator for deployed agents. Her café became a meeting place for Sussex agents transiting through Paris. There, they could get new radio codes, funds, radio sets, etc. All the equipment was stored in the cellar of the café. Madame Andrée was affectionately called "la Maman" (Mummy) by all the "Sussex".

When liberation came, this café was renamed "Café Sussex"; it was repainted and the British and American members of Sussex insisted to foot the bill. After the war, it kept its role as a meeting place for former agents who all remained very close to "la Maman". Until her death in 1988, on the first Friday of every month, she always had a table ready for the former Sussex agents, no matter what happened. Andrée Goubillon was a Knight in the order of the Légion d'honneur and she also had received the Croix de Guerre 1939-1945.

# Tribute to the "Sussex"

Once the war was over, the American authorities who wanted to pay tribute to all the Sussex agents wrote the following: "*These agents, all of them French, trained by the British Intelligence Service and the American OSS, who had been parachuted in order to operate in many different regions North of the river Loire, provided the supreme Allied commander with accurate intelligence on the enemy order of battle, the location and movements of its "Panzer" or infantry divisions, the activity of its airfields, the location of its supply, ammunition and petrol dumps including the V1 flying bombs and this on a daily basis. This constant flow of information allowed SHAEF to take crucial strategic decisions and to bring bombardment assets on to the right targets.*"

Colonel Francis Pickens Miller, in his foreword to "Colonel Rémy's" book Mémoires d'un Agent Secret de la France Libre, wrote the following on the Sussex plan:

"*The occasion which led to the meeting between "Rémy", the British officer who signed the second volume of his memories with the alias "Wagon" and the American officer I then was led to a splendid example of cooperation between the services of three different nations striving towards a common goal. Each was to play its own and distinct part in the planning and conduct of the operations. But it was the French who carried out the field tasks. When talking about intelligence, the agent in the field is the defining factor. Planning can be perfect, equipment faultless, time and luck can be on your side but it is the field agent, and the field agent only who will decide if the mission is a success or a failure. The supreme quality of this agent lies in his character.*

*I am at a loss for words when I think about the qualities of the men, women, young men and young women who departed on operational missions in support of our common goal. Their patriotism was of the purest form and the courage they showed will not be surpassed by any other. Torture had a way of revealing the true nature of a character; in this operation, that we were commanding, not a single agent revealed the name of one of his comrades under torture, not one! In this harsh and glorious command of these men and women who accepted the supreme sacrifice without ever faltering lays the hope which can be placed in to the future of France, a future which, I dare say as an American citizen, is the future of us all.*"

1. Colonel HENDERSON — 2. Capitaine WINGATE — 3. Capitaine YVONNEC
4. Colonel LEFEBVRE — 5. Colonel SAUBESTRE — 6. Lieutenant CAUMONT
7. Capitaine LE TEYRAC — 8. Capitaine BECHTEL — 9. Lieutenant GAUTHIER
10. Lieutenant CHAROT — 11. Lieutenant VALLADE — 12. Lieutenant TRAL
13. Lieutenant GUÉROULT — 14. Lieutenant LATOUR — 15. Lieutenant CLAUZEL
16. Lieutenant SAUVAGNIAC — 17. Lieutenant LESCOUR — 18. Lieutenant PICOT
19. Lieutenant ALIBERT — 20. Lieutenant COULON — 21. Lieutenant CORNU
22. MICMIC — 23. Lieutenant MEYNIEL — 24. Lieutenant LEBEL
25. Lieutenant JOURDET — 26. Lieutenant COLIN — 27. Lieutenant GEAY
28. Lieutenant GARETTE — 29. Capitaine GUYADER — 30. Madame GOUBILLON

C. THOORENS

129

# THE PROUST PLAN

BCRA, OSSEX

*The Proust insignia of Lieutenant Jacques Suissa (n°21). This insignia was produced at the same time as the Sussex badge and probably by the same engraver. Some, like this copy, were individually numbered. About 70 such insignias were produced.*
*(Sussex collection picture)*

As a sideshow to the Sussex plan and based loosely on the same principle, a secondary plan named the Proust plan was devised.

While the Sussex plan had already been launched for several months and had entered its operational phase, the American staff realised that it was likely that the Allied forces would meet very severe difficulties after the landing in France. It was then decided to reinforce the number of intelligence gathering teams operating in country. The exact tasks and missions were not yet defined but the plan was to fit into the frame of the gigantic Operation Overlord.

A secret BCRA memo (N° 379D/BCRAL), dated 11 February 1944 coming from the BCRA London

office and bound for the BCRA Algiers office reported the existence of this new plan and gave a brief description of it.

Memo for Captain Landrieux :
"The American authorities came to tell me about the creation, alongside the trilateral Sussex and Jedburgh plans, of a Proust plan designed to prepare about fifty agents in order to insert or parachute them behind German lines after the establishment of a bridgehead in France.
The Proust plan is a bilateral Franco-American organisation known to the British but in which they do not wish to get involved. American Army Colonel Neave will be in command of this organisation. A telegram has already been sent to Algiers in order to report on the creation of this new plan and to request the necessary manpower. The Americans are considering recruiting agents that failed selection (1). Please find enclosed a first list of personnel we should consider recruiting.

*Opposite.*
**Cloth "Infanterie de l'Air" para wings belonging to Jacques Suissa.**
*(Sussex collection picture)*

*Below.*
**Jacques Suissa's bullion Free French para wings.**
*(Sussex collection picture)*

*Opposite.*
**Three pages of the syllabus of the training course taught to the Sussex agents in St Alban.**
*(Sussex collection picture)*

AIR SYLLABUS.

1.

LECTURE 1. Importance of air intelligence.
State of the Luftwaffe
Organisation of the Luftwaffe, including Staffel-Gruppe-Geschwader-Fliegerkorps.
Methods of obtaining Order of Battle information.

LECTURE 2. Description and identification of aircraft.
Use of symbolic code.

LECTURE 3. Aircraft identification marks.
W/T reports on Order of Battle information, with examples.

LECTURE 4. W/T reports on:
a) Movements of formations;
b) Changes in aerodrome installations and defences;
c) Damage to aerodromes by air bombardment;
d) Damage by air bombardment to military objectives other than aerodromes.
Examples of reports will be given in each case.

LECTURE 5. Radiolocation and beam installations.
Importance, both for offensive and defensive operations.
Description of R.D.F. and beam installations.
Reports on R.D.F. and beam installations.

Period 1. Introduction.
Demonstration of efficiency of the Meth...
Basic blows
a) edge of the hand
b) chin jab
c) side kick (one foot)
d) flying jump (both feet)
e) knee

Period 2. Review.
Breaking wrist and throat holds (one hand...

Period 3. Review.
Breaking hair hold.
Breaking Front Bear Hug (over and under arms)
Alternative over-arm release.

Period 4. Review.
Breaking Rear Bear Hug (over and under arms)
Alternative over-arm release.

Period 5. Review.
Application of thumb hold and sentry hold.
Japanese stranglehold.

Period 6. Handcuff hold.
Bent arm hold.
Head hold.
Review.

Review.
Throws (hip, wrist, back)
Matchbox attack
Newspaper attack
Double ear blow.

Review.
Getting up from ground
Break-aways from "come along" holds.

Review.
Stick or cane attack
How to hold the Commando knife.

Review.
Use of the Commando knife.
Disarming the enemy of pistol.

REVIEW.

CLOSE COMBAT

LECTURE 1. Introduction
Organisation of German Army - I.

LECTURE 2. Organisation of German Army - II.

LECTURE 3. Organisation of German Army - III.

LECTURE 4. Static Reports.

LECTURE 5. Defences.

LECTURE 6. Demolitions.

LECTURE 7. Depots and parks.
Communications.

LECTURE 8. Movement Reports
Road and rail movements.

LECTURE 9. Identifications - I.
H.Q. Flags
Vehicle Markings.

LECTURE 10. Identifications - II.
W.H. Uniforms.

LECTURE 11. Identifications - III.
Mountain formations
Tank formations
Waffen S.S.

LECTURE 12. Identifications - IV.
W.L. Uniforms
Parachute Troops.

LECTURE 13. Identifications - V.
W.M. Uniforms
Para-military Formations.

LECTURE 14. Equipment - I.
A.A. and Anti-Tank guns.

LECTURE 15. Equipment - II.
Artillery weapons.

LECTURE 16. Equipment - III.
Half-tracked vehicles.
Armoured cars.

LECTURE 17. Equipment - IV.
S.P. artillery.

LECTURE 18. Equipment - V.
Tanks.

4.12.43.

You are requested to locate those individuals and to stop any "return to unit" procedure of those who have failed selection for the different plans until Colonel Neave has examined them. *The Americans have provided us with a house and instructors are ready to receive volunteers as of the 1st of March.*

*The Proust plan is an intelligence-gathering plan. Signed: Major Manuel, BCRAL chief"*

Some more information on the Proust plan can be found in another memo also signed by Major Manuel and sent three weeks later to General d'Astier, military delegate of the Comité d'action en France (memo DGSS/BCRAL N° 1834/GA/EM/S/A), dated du 6 mars 1944.

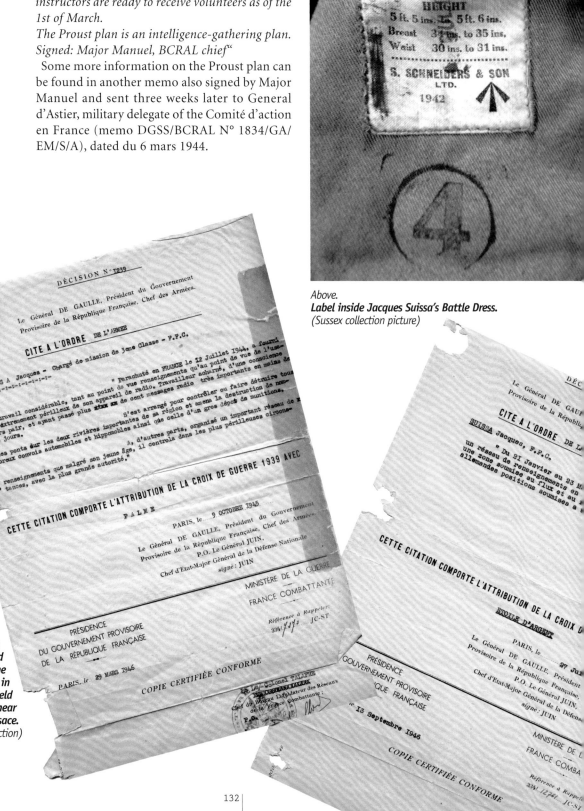

*Above.*
**Label inside Jacques Suissa's Battle Dress.**
*(Sussex collection picture)*

*Opposite.*
**Two citations for Jacques Suissa's Croix de Guerre (a palm and a Silver Star) awarded for two different missions : one in the Châteauroux region and the other during the counter-offensive led in January 1945 by Field Marshal Von Rundstedt near Haguenau in Alsace.**
*(Sussex collection)*

*Opposite.*
*Jacques Suissa's Battle Dress wit the Free French para wings (8 risers type) and, on the left sleeve, a pair of British para wings ; on the right pocket, the Proust insignia and on the left the ribbon of the American Silver Star. Underneath it, a small metal version of the FAFL badge. A pair of metal "France" titles and the shoulder slides of a Second Lieutenant can also be seen.*
*(Collection Sussex)*

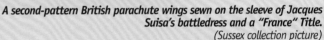

A second-pattern British parachute wings sewn on the sleeve of Jacques Suisa's battledress and a "France" Title.
(Sussex collection picture)

*Above.*
**Lieutenant Jacques Suissa a.k.a Grenier, the radio operator of the "Midiron" Proust mission. On this picture, which was taken just after the end of the war, Jacques Suissa wears the Croix de Guerre with 3 citations, the médaille des évadés (escapee medal) and the Silver Star. He wears a red beret and the newly issued 1946 pattern French metal para wings can be seen.**
(Sussex collection picture)

*Opposite.*
**OSS holster for the .32 calibre Colt pistol.**
(Sussex collection picture)

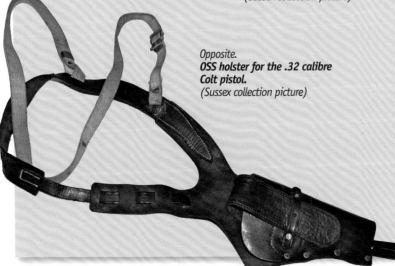

# 1944

"Following your D/A4/R memo dated 24 February 1944 with regards to the Proust plan, it is my duty to report that the American special services have requested to be provided with fifty volunteers or more in order to deploy them from D-day onwards. The Proust plan, which is a sequel to the Sussex plan, aims at training and then deploying in the future American area of operation agents that have not been integrated in the Sussex plan because they failed to meet the academic standards.

The main goal of the Proust plan is to prepare intelligence-gathering agents but it does not discount direct action entirely.

The candidates are progressively and thoroughly trained in excellent conditions in a school organised by the OSS in Horsham (Sussex)…"

know how they now would be employed in this new plan. The uncertainty led to considerable frustration on their part; these men felt that they

Above.
**Jacques Suissa's US M1 helmet bearing the American rank of a Second Lieutenant. American rank insignias were often worn by French agents operating as part of the Sussex et Proust plans for the OSS.**
(Sussex collection picture)

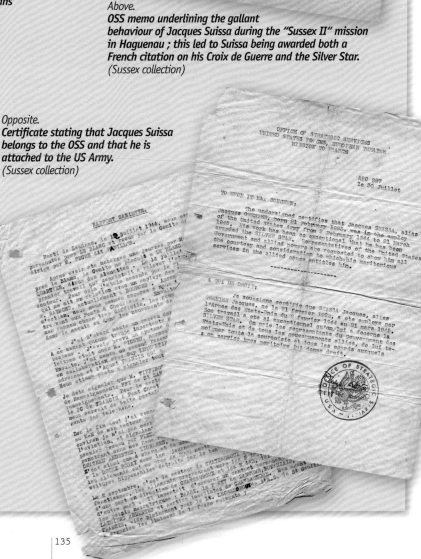

Above.
**OSS memo underlining the gallant behaviour of Jacques Suissa during the "Sussex II" mission in Haguenau ; this led to Suissa being awarded both a French citation on his Croix de Guerre and the Silver Star.**
(Sussex collection)

Opposite.
**Certificate stating that Jacques Suissa belongs to the OSS and that he is attached to the US Army.**
(Sussex collection)

had been selected for some sort of a sideshow designed for undesirable Sussex agents. Moral had been hit and I had a few disciplinary cases."

Some tough action was required and it was only after the agents left Ringway after having gone through the parachute qualification course that moral markedly improved. The training phase of the roughly fifty selected agents started in mid-April 1944.

# The training phase

Since Sussex had started operating in France, it freed some American instructors who then became available for Proust. The agents of those two missions received the same training.

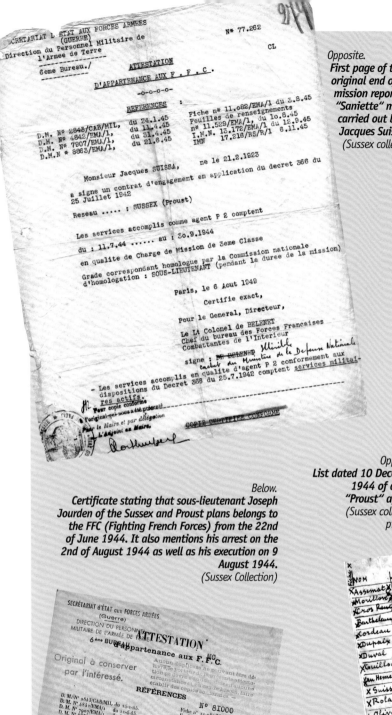

*Opposite.*
**First page of the original end of mission report of the "Saniette" mission carried out by Jacques Suissa.**
*(Sussex collection)*

It took place in Drungwick Manor (codename Aera B), a gorgeous XIIIth Century building which had been renovated in the XIXth Century by American theatre producer Gilbert Miller, its owner.

The officers in charge of training were housed in the castle where the Mess an administrative services were also located while the volunteers were put up in tents pegged in the vast park which also was used as a training area for hand to hand combat, physical training, tactical shooting and demolition training. The weekly reports drafted by Major Dutey, the French deputy to Colonel Neave, mentioned field exercises with the British secret services as well as practical exercises on the preparation of a cover story, on the operation of the different radio sets, on vehicle driving, weapons recognition, etc.

On 21 May 1944, the Proust plan had strength of 65 men. On 7 June, Lieutenant-colonel Booth

*Below.*
**Certificate stating that sous-lieutenant Joseph Jourden of the Sussex and Proust plans belongs to the FFC (Fighting French Forces) from the 22nd of June 1944. It also mentions his arrest on the 2nd of August 1944 as well as his execution on 9 August 1944.**
*(Sussex Collection)*

*Opposite.*
**List dated 10 December 1944 of all the "Proust" agents.**
*(Sussex collection picture)*

took command of the Freehold school and Neave was recalled to the OSS offices in London. Thanks to Major Dutey's notes, it is possible to say with confidence that in the best possible scenario, no more than 65 men followed Proust training. All of them did not complete the full curriculum and some only spent a few days in training. Of note is the fact that 14 agents were posted to the Sussex plan including Guy Mocquet, Lucien Bignon ("Daru" mission) and Mario Faivre ("Velours" mission).

If one adds to those figures the few French BCRA/OSS liaison officers, a total figure of less than 80 Frenchmen assigned to the Proust plan can be retained. Most of the missions did a parachute insertion, except two teams that had maritime insertions via PT Boats courtesy of the OSS maritime section and two others that were landed in "pick up" operations.

*Opposite.*
**Joseph Jourden a.k.a "Jean-Marie Stur" of the "Girafe" Proust mission. He covertly arrived by sea in France, landing with J.M. Robleu, (an alias for R. Reitzer) in the Morlaix region near the pointe de Beg-an-Fry in Britanny on 25 June 1944.**
*(UNC Le Conquet and Roger Coguiec source, www. francaislibres.net website)*

*Below.*
**List of the agents having operated in support of the "Hugo". mission.**
*(Sussex collection)*

À le Lieut-Colonel M Henderson.                          PARIS, le 17 Octobre 1944.

Mon Colonel,

Cette lettre vous est addressee au nom des "Sussex" qui depuis pres d'un an maintenant ont eu l'honneur et la chance d'etre sous vos ordres. Des notre arrivee a l'ecole nous avions apprecie le chef que vous etes et surtout la grande comprehension et meme la sympathie que vous nous prodiguiez, et depuis lors chacun d'entre nous ne peut se souvenir qu'avec emotion et gratitude de la part que vous avez pris dans nos efforts. A une epoque ou notre pays etait prive de sa liberte vous avez tout fait en Angleterre pour que nous retrouvions une atmosphere agreable, et aujourd'hui que grace a l'enseignement recu sous vos directives, nous avons pu s'accomplir avec succes, vous avez tenu vous meme a regler les differents problemes souleves en France par notre action.

Pour tout cela, mon Colonel, nous vous remercions; mais nous attendons encore une chose de vous: nous desirerions poursuivre cette guerre sous vos ordres afin que cet esprit "Sussex" puisse nous servir dans les differentes taches qui nous seront assignees. Nous desirerions que cette unitie Franco-Brittanique nee a Prae Wood se poursuive, en meme temps que se poursuivra cette union entre nous tous.

Dans l'espoir que notre desir trouvera une realisation prochaine, veuillez recevoir, mon Colonel, l'expression de nos sentiments d'attachement les plus respectueux.

| | | | | | |
|---|---|---|---|---|---|
| Adam | Beaufils | Clauzel | Gauthier | Lebel | Petitjean |
| Aury | Bechtel | Collard | Goly | Laugier | Philippe |
| Beignet | Beon | Corbin | Guichard | Laune | Picot |
| Berlioz | Bordier | Coulombel | Garette | Laurent | Pierlot |
| Berthet | Bouchot | Coulon | Geay | Lebaud | Regnier |
| Bertin | Breguet | Cremieux | Greleur | Leblanc | Rigal |
| Bertrand | Bugeaud | D'Arsac | Grosbot | Marchand, J. | Roux |
| Bessonne | Bordes | Delpeyre | Grandet | Malbrunet | Rogier |
| Blanc | Boudemange | Desmarchais | Jourdet | Meyniel | Sagan |
| Boissier | Bousquet | Desnoyers | Joyeuse | Moutier | Sauvagnac |
| Cabossel | Chaloner | Deniel | Kergour | Massonet | Schupo |
| Carlier | Caumont | Digne | Fenocque | Montjean | Sandeau |
| Charot | Colin | Dubost | Landren | Morgen | Surville |
| Cornu | Crepy | Dujardin | Latour | Morval | Thenet |
| Duvalet | Sven | Fouquet | Laville | Nedelec | Tral |
| Olivier | Piron | Pradel | Puissegur | Pautard | Treville |
| Thibert | Verneuil | Vernez | Vermuge | Vallade | |

137

*The first mission, "Girafe", was also the only one to suffer the loss of an agent, namely Joseph Jourden a.k.a "Jean-Marie Stur":*

Having joined the Sussex plan under the name of "Jean-Marie Stur" and having finally been integrated into the Proust plan as part of the "Girafe"mission, he was covertly landed with "J.M. Robleu" (real name R. Reitzer) in the Morlaix region of Brittany in the vicinity of the pointe de Beg an Fry, on 25 June 1944. His mission was to gather intelligence on enemy strength, equipment and dispositions and to identify the German units that were likely to oppose the Allied forces that had already landed in Normandy on 6th June.

"La girafe à la laryngite" (the girafe has a laryngitis) was the coded sentence that the London radio had to broadcast in order to warn Joseph Jourden that soon a message was going to come his way. This was an allusion to his raspy voice. Until 9th August 1944, he managed to escape German Direction Finding efforts. Basing his researches on the testimony of monsieur Ruppe, the priest of the Ploujean parish, another clergyman, chanoine Pérenes, wrote a study named *Aviateurs alliés et journées tragiques de la Libération dans quelques localités du Finistère* (published in 1946), which detailed the string of events that led to the death of Joseph Jourden :

"On 8 August 1944, American troops had gone through Plouigneau without firing a shot. On 9 August, an isolated German detachment, about 200-strong with some field guns and other weapons entered the small town. The FFI tried to push them back but they were not in sufficient numbers. Five patriots (Joseph Jourden and four others who had arrived on the main square in a car festooned with Allied flags and cross of Lorraine) were arrested and shot on the plaza in front of the church". The French and American official reports on these events were more accurate; they underlined the fact Joseph Jourden had been captured by a German detachment on 9 August, that he was tortured for four hours on the village square and that, in spite of the atrocious pain he refused to talk, displaying an incredible courage. Not managing to put him back on his legs, the Germans finally shot him in the head.

On the same day, R. Reitzer, both the teammate and the friend of Jourden, informed his family that he had died; his remains were taken to his sister in the city of Morlaix. An armed American soldier was placed at the church's door and a detachment composed of FFIs and American soldiers escorted the hearse to the cemetery where Joseph Jourden was given full military honours. A commemorative plaque can be seen to these days near the monument to the dead of Plouigneau. Joseph Jourden was posthumously decorated with the cross of chevalier de la Légion d'honneur; he also received the Croix de Guerre with palm, the médaille de la Résistance Française, as well as a posthumous Distinguished Service Cross from the Americans. An American officer awarded the DSC to Joseph Jourden's father on 1 June 1945 in front of the townhall of the city of Le Conquet. The main street of Le Conquet has been bearing the name of Joseph Jourden since the 6th of June 1945. The "Midiron" mission was a typical Proust mission. In liaison with the maquis, the agents were to report on German movements towards the Belfort Gap to the US 3rd Army. The mission chief was Bougier a.k.a "Bricard", a.k.a "Bartoldi". The mission was parachuted on 12 July 1944 in Douadic (in the Indre département). The main task was to report on enemy convoys in the areas of Angoulême, Poitiers, Le Blanc, Limoges, Châteauvieux and Dijon.

This mission was composed of several teams:
- "Saniette" with Jacques Suissa a.k.a "Grenier", parachuted on 12 July in Le Blanc at the same time as "Charlus" ;
- "Congé" with Georges Cordeau a.k.a "Courtois", parachuted during the night of the 7 to the 8 of August. It established contact with the Limoges area maquis in order to conduct intelligence-gathering missions in the cities of Angoulême and Poitiers;
- "Poil" with René Gros a.k.a "Bordenave", who conducted an intelligence gathering missions which led to a bombardment by American assets which destroyed an important enemy concentration.

The "Midiron" agents sent a total of 151 messages to Victor (the OSS central radio station in the United Kingdom) where they were collated, processed and dispatched towards the 7th and 9th US Armies. By the end of the Summer of 1944, the American bridgehead on the continent was considered as strong enough to justify the end of both the Proust and Sussex missions.

Thus, after the Normandy landings, Proust was used as a manpower pool for the operations that could not be carried out by Sussex. At the end of the month of August, the few remaining agents in training in Drungwick Manor were sent to France. They were either posted to the "field detachment" (SI/OSS) that went along with the 3rd and 7th US Armies in order to support them in their intelligence gathering tasks or to the OSS base in recently liberated Paris. Most returned to the DGER which offered them other

missions. The men and women who had been the heart and soul of the Sussex, Proust and Jedburgh plans all then went their different ways. The DGER seconded many of them for counter-intelligence tasks to the nineteen screening centres for former French POWs and deportees. All the recently returned displaced personnel, regardless of their nationalities, were subjected to security interrogation as the security services tried to both verify their personal history and extract strategic, political or economical information from them.

The Proust and Sussex plans were well and truly over. Other intelligence or security (Hébé, Nulton, Nicotine, etc.) missions were to soon use the same personnel. Some left for the Far East with the Commando Conus or Kay2...but then, this is a different story!

*Top to bottom: British parachute wings, British Parachute Regiment beret badge minus its crown as worn by French paratroopers, printed "France" titles, 1st Free French Division (1ere DFL) sleeve insignia, metal "France" titles, and American parachute wings. (Sussex collection picture)*

*Capitaine Pierre Vergès d'Espagne, alias "Le Teyrac".*

*Lieutenant Edmond Delaplanque, alias "Cornu".*

*Lieutenant Charles Darquès, alias "Fouquet".*

*Lieutenant Jean Burtey, alias "D'Arzac".*

*Lieutenant Julien Fayet, alias "Latour".*

*Lieutenant Gabriel Guenard, alias "Laugier".*

*Lieutenant Auberger, alias "Adam".*

*Lieutenant Pierre Lecomte, alias "Meyniel".*

*Lieutenant Lucien Millet, alias "Marchand".*

*Lieutenant Jean-Yves Quentel, alias "Nedelec".*

*Lieutenant Quillent, alias "Malbrunay".*

*Lieutenant Bernard Roupain, alias "François".*

Lieutenant Jean Lart, alias "Tral".

Lieutenant Mario Faivre, alias "Régnier".

Lieutenant Jean-Marie de Beaucorp, alias "Kergou".

Lieutenant Bissey Jean-Pierre, alias "Even".

Lieutenant Alibert.

Lieutenant Claude Guyomar, alias "Goudelin".

Lieutenant François Humbert, alias "Bouchot".

Lieutenant Brunet, alias "Digne" et M. Labeste FFI.

Lieutenant Paul Sautière, alias "Bordier".

Capitaine Guyader.

Lieutenant Gueudelot, alias "Greleur".

Lieutenant Degorse, alias « Bessonne ».

# GLOSSARY

**Abwehr :** German armed forces intelligence service

**BBC :** British Broadcasting Corporation; British state radio

**BCRA :** Bureau central de renseignement et d'action; Free French secret services

**B.M.T. :** Bataillon de Marche du Tchad (colonial infantry unit recruited in Chad)

**B.R.A.L. :** Bureau de Recherche et d'Action de Londres (London-based intelligence and direct action bureau of the BCRA)

**CFLN :** Comité Français de Libération Nationale ; Free French national liberation committee

**CIA :** (Central Intelligence Agency) : American intelligence agency ; the successor of the OSS

**DCA :** Défense contre avions ; air-defense artillery

**DGER :** Direction générale des Etudes et Recherches (ex DGSS) : general directorate for studies and research (formerly known as the DGSS)

**DGSS :** Direction Générale des Services Spéciaux ; general directorate of special services

**DZ :** Dropping Zone

**ETO :** European Theater of Operations

**ETOUSA :** European Theather of Operations, US Army

**FAFL :** Forces Aérienne Française Libres : Free French air force

**FFC :** Forces Françaises Combattantes ; Fighting French forces

**FFI :** Forces Françaises de l'Intérieur ; French forces of the interior ; the gathering, under the authority of Général De Gaulle, of most non-Communist résistance forces

**FFL :** Forces Française Libre : Free French Forces

**FLAK :** Fliegerabwehrkanone, German air defense artillery

**FNFL :** Forces Navales Française Libre ; Free French naval forces

**FTP :** Francs-tireurs et partisans : French Communist résistance

**G-2 :** general name for the intelligence branch

**GO :** OSS Operational Groups

**GQG :** Grand quartier général, general headquarters

**Lt :** Lieutenant

**MCR-1 :** Radio set used by the Sussex missions to listen to BBC "broadcast" messages

**MI-5 :** (Military Intelligence-5) : British intelligence service tasked with domestic counter-intelligence

**MI-6 :** (Military Intelligence-6) : British intelligence service tasked with foreign counter-intelligence

**MK 7 :** Radio set placed in a suitcase used by the Sussex missions

**NARA :** National Archives and Records Administration: US National Archives

**OS** (Special Operations, SO) : the OSS Special Operations branch

**OSS :** Office of Strategic Services, American intelligence service

**"QB" paper :** (Quick Burning) : Paper made with a powder base and which self destructed instantly when exposed to a flame

**PC :** Poste de commandement ; command post

**Pilule L** (Lethal) : Cyanide pill

**Pilule K** (Knock-out) : sleeping pill

**PZKW** (Panzerkampfwagen) : German name for armoured fighting vehicles

**QG :** Quartier general; headquarters

**RAF :** Royal Air Force

**RSA :** Régiment de Spahis Algériens (light cavalry unit recruited from French North African colonies)

**S2 :** staff officer in charge of military intelligence

**SAS :** Special Air Service : 1 and 2 SAS were British, 3 and 4 SAS were Free French and 5 SAS was composed of Belgian volunteers

**SHAEF** Supreme Headquarters Allied Expeditionary Forces

**SI** Secret Intelligence : secret intelligence, one of the OSS branches

**SIS** Secret Intelligence Service : British secret intelligence service

**SOE :** Special Operations Executive

**SR :** Service de renseignement ; French intelligence service ;

**SS :** Schutztaffel : a military unit of the Nazi party that served as Hitler's bodyguard and as a special police force

**SSTR-1 :** A transceiver placed in a suitcase ; often used by Sussex missions

**STO :** The Service du travail obligatoire (Compulsory Work Service) was the forced enlistment and deportation of hundreds of thousands of French workers to Nazi Germany in order to work as forced labour for the German war effort. French males born between 1920-1922 were concerned by this measure

**S-PHONE :** an ultra high frequency duplex radio telephone system used by agents working behind enemy lines to communicate with friendly aircraft

**T Force :** attached to the 12th Army group, the T-Forces was ordered to identify, secure, guard and exploit valuable and special information, including documents, equipment and persons of value to the Allied armies

**V1** (Vergeltungswaffe 1) : Fi-103 V-1 flying bomb also known as "reprisal weapon #1"

**V2** (Vergeltungswaffe 2) : A4 balistic missile also known as "reprisal weapon #2"

*Jacques Suiswsa's Free French parachute wings.* (Sussex collection picture)

# BIBLIOGRAPHY

*Souvenirs d'une mission à Blois by Georges Soulier.*
*Mémoires d'un agent secret de la France Libre par Rémy (Presses Pocket publishing).*
*Paris 1944, Les Enjeux de la Libération par Arthur Funk (Albin Michel publishing).*
*Revue de la France Libre, spécial 50e Anniversaire de l'Appel du 18 juin 1940.*
*Revue de la France Libre, n° 310 spécial 60e Anniversaire*
*Revue Icare, Aviateurs et Résistants, tome II et III by Louis Guyomard.*
*OSS, La guerre secrète en France par Fabrizio Calvi (Hachette publishing).*
*Les Mains Jointes by Rémy (Raoul Solar publishing)*
*La guerre secrète contre Hitler by William Casey (Robert Laffont publishing)*
*The Secret War Report of the O.S.S. by Anthony Cave Brown (Berkley Publishing Corporation)*

*NARA, Washington DC (National Archives)*
*Notes à propos de 1944 by Mario Faivre (Gazelles Editions publishing) with the kind authorization of the author*
*Un certain Louis Bonnet by J.J. Schumacher restricted distribution for the Amicale du Plan Sussex, with the kind authorization of Jean-Jacques Schumacher.*
*UNC Le Conquet (for Joseph Jourden)*
*Roger Coguiec (for Joseph Jourden) (www.francaislibres.net) website*
*Symboles & Traditions, bulletin N°176 by Serge Larcher*
*Mission "Daru" by Raymond Mocquet.*

# ACKNOWLEDGEMENT

With my heartfelt thanks to all the former members of "Sussex" and to their families for their precious assistance and the loan and gift of equipment and documents as well as for their testimonies:

Colette Bechtel, Jacques Bignon, Lucette Clopet, Jacques Coulon et Jean-Pierre Coulon, Patrice Ducasse, Roger Goguiec, François de Gombert, Olivier de Gombert, Mario Faivre, Pierre Fauroux, Madame Jacqueline Guillebaud, Madame Marie Claude Maslard, Emile Gendarme, Louis Guyomard et Anne-Marie Guyomard, Dominique William, Patrick William et Tilly, Madame Lart, Jean-Pierre Psaltis et Fréderic Psaltis, Yves Quentel, Pierre Ravarre, René Razaire, Arlette Sadoun, Paul, Sautière, Georges Soulier, Jean-Jacques Suissa, Pierre Tillet, Henri Tosi, Jill Henderson, Jeannette Guyot, Laetitia Garçon, Michel Vergès d'Espagne, Christian Viard, Guy Wingate et Kate Wingate, Stéphanie Quantrell-Park et Bonnie Friedman, Patricia Cleveland Peck, Jean-Claude Augst, Jean-Jacques Schumacher, Jean-Louis Perquin, Serge Larcher, Ronald Hirlé, Eric Micheletti, Eric Valette d'Osia, Vladimir Trouplin, Sébastien Albertelli, Philippe Chapillon, Georges Ducreuzet, Bernard Riff, Nathalie Genet-Rouffiac, Jean Klein, Maryvonne Kientz, Eric Kauffmann et Carine Lemarchand.

A heartfelt thanks to my wife Evelyne who gave me full and unwavering support in this long undertaking to pay tribute to the "Sussex".

## IN THE SAME COLLECTION

**LES OPÉRATEURS RADIO CLANDESTINS**

**THE CLANDESTINE RADIO OPERATORS**

**LES PARACHUTAGES ET ATTERRISSAGES CLANDESTINS TOME I**

**CLANDESTINE PARACHUTE AND PICK-UP OPERATIONS VOLUME I**

**AGENTS SECRETS FRANCE LIBRE**

**FREE FRENCH SECRET AGENTS**

**THIS BOOK WAS EDITED BY ERIC MICHELETTI.
DESIGN AND LAYOUT CARINE LEMARCHAND.
TRANSLATED BY GEORGES BRASPART.**

*Histoire & Collections*

5, avenue de la République
F-75541 Paris Cédex 11
Tel: 01 40 21 18 20 / Fax: 01 47 00 51 11
w w w . h i s t o i r e e t c o l l e c t i o n s . c o m

This book has been designed, typed, laid-out and processed by Histoire & Collections on fully integrated computer equipment.

Print by Calidad Grafica, Spain, European Union, November 2013.